Minorities in U.S. Institutions of Higher Education

Frank Brown
Madelon D. Stent

The Praeger Special Studies program—
utilizing the most modern and efficient book
production techniques and a selective
worldwide distribution network—makes
available to the academic, government, and
business communities significant, timely
research in U.S. and international economic, social, and political development.

Minorities in U.S. Institutions of Higher Education

101832

PRAEGER SPECIAL STUDIES IN U.S. ECONOMIC, SOCIAL, AND POLITICAL ISSUES

Praeger Publishers   New York   London

Library of Congress Cataloging in Publication Data

Brown, Frank, 1935-
    Minorities in U.S. institutions of higher education.

    (Praeger special studies in U.S. economic, social,
and political issues)
    Bibliography: p.
    Includes index.
    1. Minorities—Education (Higher)—United States.
I. Stent, Madelon D., joint author. II. Title.
LC3731.B69   371.9'7'0973   75-19768
ISBN 0-275-55540-2

PRAEGER PUBLISHERS
200 Park Avenue, New York, N.Y. 10017, U.S.A.

Published in the United States of America in 1977
by Praeger Publishers, Inc.

789   038   987654321

Printed in the United States of America

Once every decade, efforts are made by the federal government to collect demographic data. These data are rather general, except for a count of the population by cities, states, regions, and the nation as a whole. Although more specific data on higher education by race and ethnicity are included in the decennial survey by the United States Bureau of the Census, the task of compiling data on minorities in higher education involves gathering data from a variety of sources: the Bureau of the Census, special survey by state and federal agencies, professional associations, surveys funded by private foundations, and occasionally information compiled by individual researchers.

This book is a compilation of data from these sources. <u>Minorities in U.S. Institutions of Higher Education</u> combines into one source data from the Office for Civil Rights (OCR), the Census Bureau, and the National Center for Education Statistics and other data. In the absence of supportive data, discussion, and analysis, enrollment data alone are disastrously inadequate; they have too often created a false sense of increased opportunities and achievement for minorities in higher education. This book attempts to clearly present the facts to reveal if and how minorities in higher education have progressed, or if they have regressed.

Data collection is a big business and an important one for any organization, government, or sub-government unit. Data are used to evaluate organizational inputs, throughputs, and outputs. They provide accountability and measure productivity. They can be used to plan future courses of action and as a bench mark to evaluate social justice among different groups within an organization or governmental unit. In many instances, as with public institutions of higher education, data on enrollment by race and ethnicity may serve a dual function such as the evaluation of the college as a viable formal organization, and as a government agency. In a real sense all higher education institutions in the United States are governmental units since almost all, public and private, receive government funds, and students enrolled in both types may receive government support. The only real difference between private and public colleges is the relative level of public support.

The presence of adequate data on minority enrollment in higher education should make for more positive and rational planning by colleges to better serve the minority population. While having adequate data on minorities in higher education is no guarantee that colleges and universities will try to improve conditions for minorities, without adequate data they will be less inclined to improve conditions for minorities. We hope that this book will stimulate efforts by the government and its sub-units to produce better data on the status of minorities in higher education.

This study would not have been possible without the assistance and cooperation of many individuals and agencies. We would like to express our appreciation to each and every one for their assistance. While it is not possible to list the names of everyone who made a contribution, we wish to thank Dr. Benjamin F. Payton of the Ford Foundation whose faith and financial support made the whole project possible; the Rockefeller Foundation for its Villa Serbelloni Scholar Award which provided the intellectual atmosphere for study; Mr. Carlos Vernon, graduate student at the State University of New York at Buffalo, for his editorial assistance with the manuscript; Ms. Elaine Raimonds for her patience and diligence in typing the manuscript; and the librarians and staff of the College of Mount St. Vincent for the use of their library.

We also extend our sincere appreciation to those who reviewed the manuscript and gave us helpful feedback: Dr. Bruce Fleming, U.S. Office of Education; Mrs. Patricia Locke, Western Interstate Commission for Higher Education; Dr. Stephen J. Wright, College Entrance Examination Board; Dr. Frank Bonilla, City University of New York; Dr. Arturo Madrid, University of Minnesota, Twin Cities; and Dr. Lucie C. Hirata, University of California at Los Angeles.

Finally, we wish to express our deep appreciation to our families, especially our spouses, Joan and Teddy, for their sacrifices while we worked on this project.

CONTENTS

Page

PREFACE   v

LIST OF TABLES   ix

Chapter

1   INTRODUCTION   1

    Organization of the Book   2
    Methodology and Data Analysis   7
    Summary   11

2   THE BENEFITS OF A COLLEGE EDUCATION   13

    Why Attend College?   13
    Who Attends College?   16
    What Are the Opportunities to Attend College?   18

3   UNDERGRADUATE ENROLLMENT   21

    Native Americans   21
    Blacks   28
    Asian Americans   39
    Hispanic Americans   45

4   BACHELOR'S DEGREES EARNED   59

    Blacks   63
    Native Americans   66
    Hispanic Americans   67
    Asian Americans   68

5   ENGINEERING AND PHARMACY   69

    Engineering   69
    Pharmacy   78

6   GRADUATE AND PROFESSIONAL SCHOOL
    ENROLLMENT AND EARNED DEGREES   82

    Graduate Enrollment (Except Dental, Medical, and Law)   86
    Dental Schools   86
    Medical Schools   88
    Law Schools   93
    The Academic Doctorate   96
    Ethnic Graduate Schools and Programs   103

7   HIGHER EDUCATION ENROLLMENT IN SELECTED
    STATES   104

    California   104
    Florida   106
    Illinois   108
    New York   110
    Texas   112
    Summary   114

8   ECONOMIC INDICATORS AND THE MINORITY
    COLLEGE STUDENT   116

    Economic Indicators   116
    Educational Costs   121
    Programs for Student Assistance   130

9   MINORITY STUDENTS ON CAMPUS   137

    The Effects of Student Unrest in the 1960s   138
    A Realignment of Priorities in the 1970s ?   139
    Enrollment and Retention   141
    Black Students on Campus   142
    The Chicano Student in the 1970s   146
    Community Colleges: The Inflation Spiral
       in Higher Education   148

10 SUMMARY AND RECOMMENDATIONS   155

REFERENCES   161

SELECTED BIBLIOGRAPHY   165

INDEX   175

ABOUT THE AUTHORS   179

LIST OF TABLES

Table   Page

2.1   Education and Income in the United States, March 1974, Median Income   14

2.2   Income of Males and Schooling, 1970   15

2.3   School Enrollment and Educational Attainment of the U.S. Population by Race, 1970   17

2.4   Occupation of Employed Persons by Race, 1970, 50 States and District of Columbia   19

3.1   Native American Population of the United States, 1900 to 1970   22

3.2   Enrollment (all ages) by Types of Schools Operated by the Bureau of Indian Affairs, Fiscal Years 1973 and 1974   24

3.3   Enrollment in Schools Operated and Funded by the Bureau of Indian Affairs, Fiscal Years 1973 and 1974   25

3.4   Completions and Number of Graduates of Schools Operated by the Bureau of Indian Affairs, Fiscal Year 1974   25

3.5   Native American Undergraduate Enrollment, Summary Data   26

3.6   Black Undergraduate Enrollment, Summary Data   29

3.7   The College-Age Population by Race   32

3.8   Postsecondary School Enrollment of Persons 16 to 34 Years Old, by Type of School, 1973   34

3.9   Weighted National Norms for Universities, Fall 1974   36

3.10   College Enrollment, 3 to 34 Years Old, October 1964 to October 1974   37

Table   Page

3.11   Total Enrollment, Fall 1974, and Degrees
        Conferred, 1971–72, in U.S. Institutions
        Attended Predominantly by Black Students   38

3.12   Immigrants Born in Specified Asian Countries
        and Areas, 1972   40

3.13   Sex Ratio of Chinese in the United States, 1860–1970   41

3.14   Chinese Population in the United States, 1910–70   42

3.15   Asian American Undergraduate Enrollment,
        Summary Data   43

3.16   Hispanic American Population in the United States
        by Type of Spanish Origin, March 1975   46

3.17   Hispanic Americans in the United States and
        Selected Areas in March 1974   47

3.18   Hispanic American Population by Sex and Type of
        Spanish Origin, for the United States and Five
        Southwestern States, March 1974   49

3.19   Persons of Puerto Rican Birth or Parentage in the
        United States and in New York City, 1950–70   50

3.20   Hispanic Americans by Race, for the United
        States, 1970   51

3.21   Hispanic American Undergraduate Enrollment,
        Summary Data   53

3.22   Years of School Completed by Hispanic Americans
        14 Years Old and Over, United States, March 1974   54

3.23   Undergraduate College Enrollment of Persons 14 to
        34 Years Old by Type of College, Year, Spanish
        Origin, and Age, October 1972   56

3.24   Percent Undergraduate Enrollment, Total United
        States and Five Selected States, 1968–74   57

x

Table		Page
4.1	Estimates of Bachelor's Degrees Earned, 1968-74, from U.S. Institutions of Higher Education	60
4.2	Associate Degrees, Diplomas, and Other Awards Based on Less Than Four Years of Work Beyond High School, 50 States and District of Columbia, 1970	61
4.3	Resident Undergraduate Enrollment for Ethnic Groups by Year Enrolled, Full Time and Part Time, 50 States and District of Columbia, 1970	62
4.4	Number of Baccalaureate Degrees Awarded in Historically Black Colleges by Selected Fields, 1965-66 to 1972-73	64
4.5	Percentage of Bachelor's Degrees Awarded by Selected Fields in Historically Black Colleges and Nationally, 1965-66 to 1972-73	65
4.6	Bachelor's, Master's, and Doctor's Degrees in Ethnic Studies Conferred in U.S. Institutions of Higher Education, 1972-73 and 1973-74	66
4.7	Enrollment and Educational Attainment, Bureau of Indian Affairs Higher Education Programs, 1973 and 1974	67
5.1	Number and Percent of Minorities Enrolled in Engineering by Degree Level, Fall 1973	70
5.2	Enrollment of Blacks in Engineering by Degree Level, 1969-70 to 1973-74	71
5.3	Bachelor's Degrees in Engineering by Curriculum and Minority Status, 1974	72
5.4	Master's Degrees in Engineering by Curriculum and Minority Status, 1974	73
5.5	Doctoral Degrees in Engineering by Curriculum and Minority Status, 1974	74

Table   Page

5.6   Engineering Degrees Granted to Minorities by
       Degree Level, 1972-73 and 1973-74   75

5.7   Class Standing of Minority Engineering Students at
       148 Schools by Sex, Fall 1973   76

5.8   Estimated Enrollment and B.S. Degrees in
       Engineering Earned at U.S. Black Colleges
       and Universities, 1972-73   77

5.9   Engineering Degrees Granted to Blacks by Degree
       Level, 1968-69 to 1973-74   77

5.10   Estimates of Pharmacy Enrollment by Race and
       Ethnicity, 1972-73   79

5.11   Minorities Employed in Engineering, 1974   79

5.12   Racial/Ethnic Groups Identified in the Comprehensive
       Roster of Doctoral Scientists and Engineers, by
       Academic Year of Doctorate   80

6.1   Estimates of Graduate Enrollment in U.S. Institutions
       of Higher Education, except Law, Dental, and
       Medical, 1968, 1970, 1972, and 1974   83

6.2   Graduate School Full- and Part-Time Enrollment
       by Field of Study for Various Ethnic Groups   84

6.3   Comparison of Data Sources on 1970 Graduate
       School Enrollment in the United States, except
       Law, Dental, and Medical   85

6.4   Total Family Income of First-Year Graduate
       Students   85

6.5   Dental School Minority Enrollment   87

6.6   Enrollment in Black Dental Schools in the United
       States, 1972-73   87

6.7   Total Minority Enrollment in U.S. Medical Schools,
       1969-73   89

Table		Page
6.8	Percentage Minority Enrollment in U.S. Medical Schools, 1972–73 and 1973–74	90
6.9	Black U.S. Citizens Serving in Medical Residencies, by Specialty, as of September 1, 1973	91
6.10	Students Admitted 1971–72 to 1973–74 and Still in School in June 1974	92
6.11	Students Repeating the Academic Year, 1973–74	93
6.12	Minority Students Enrolled in Approved Law Schools, 1969–74	94
6.13	Quartile Ranking after Three Years of Study of Disadvantaged Law Students Who Started School in 1970	95
6.14	Academic Status after Three Years of Study of Disadvantaged Law Students Who Started School in 1970	95
6.15	Statistical Profile of Persons Receiving Doctoral Degrees, by Field of Study, 1972–73	97
6.16	Field of Doctorate	98
6.17	Enrollment of Minority Graduate Students: Number in Each Field of Study, Fall 1973	100
6.18	Number Receiving Doctoral Degrees in 1973, by Citizenship and Racial/Ethnic Identification	101
6.19	Doctorates Awarded in Historically Black Colleges, 1971–73	102
6.20	Professional Degrees Awarded in Historically Black Colleges in Selected Fields, 1971–73	102
7.1	College Enrollment for California and the Los Angeles SMSA, 1970	105
7.2	College Enrollment for Florida and the Miami SMSA, 1970	107

xiii

Table		Page
7.3	College Enrollment for Illinois and the Chicago SMSA, 1970	109
7.4	College Enrollment for New York and the New York City SMSA, 1970	111
7.5	College Enrollment for Texas and the Houston SMSA, 1970	113
7.6	Native American Undergraduate Enrollment from Two Data Sources: U.S. Census and OCR, 1970	115
8.1	Median Income of Families, 1964-74	117
8.2	Unemployment Rates, by Sex and Age, 1973 and 1974	117
8.3	Family Members 18 to 24 Years Old, by College Enrollment Status and Family Income, 1974	118
8.4	Persons in the United States Below the Low-Income Level, 1969-74	119
8.5	Income in 1974 of All Families and Familes with Head of Spanish Origin, United States	120
8.6	Persons by Type of Spanish Origin and Low-Income Status, United States and Five Southwestern States, 1973	120
8.7	Median Expected Educational Expenses by Type of College, Attendance Status, and Control of School, October 1973	122
8.8	Educational Expenses for Postsecondary Students by Type of School, October 1973	123
8.9	Mean Educational Costs to Undergraduates, Public and Private Institutions, by Selected Characteristics, 1974-75	123
8.10	Source and Amount of Funds Available for Undergraduate and Graduate Students, by Type and Control of Institution, 1974-75	125

Table   Page

8.11   Characteristics of All Students (Unduplicated
       Count) Receiving Aid under Office of Education
       Assistance Programs, by Type and Control of
       Institution, 1974–75   126

8.12   Percentage of Students Receiving Aid under Office
       of Education Assistance Programs, by Selected
       Characteristics of Recipients, 1974–75   128

8.13   Average Amount of Assistance Awarded under
       Office of Education Assistance Programs, by
       Control and Type of Institution, 1974–75   129

8.14   Distribution of New York Four-Year State-
       Operated Campus EOP Students, Outside of
       New York City, 1974–75   129

8.15   Percent of Undergraduate Postsecondary Students
       Expecting to Receive Income from Selected
       Sources Between July 1973 and June 1974 and
       Average Amount Received   131

8.16   Source of Income for Postsecondary Students
       16 Years Old and Over, 1973   132

8.17   Number of NDSL, SEOG, and CWS Aid Recipients
       and Amounts Spent in These Programs by
       Racial/Ethnic Distribution, Fiscal Year 1974   134

Minorities in U.S. Institutions of Higher Education

The purpose of this book is to present up-to-date data and analysis of the status of racial and ethnic minorities enrolled in institutions of higher education in the United States. This is a follow up to a 1974 publication on this subject, Minority Enrollment and Representation in Institutions of Higher Education: A Survey on Minority Students Enrollment in Colleges, Universities, Graduate and Professional Schools in 50 States and The District of Columbia (Stent and Brown 1974). The major purpose of the first study was simply to compile, in one place, available data on minority enrollment in institutions of higher education. The intent of this book is to update these data (when possible) and to provide the necessary narrative to clarify the data and to make projections and policy recommendations. We hope to add further to this book by assessing areas of college and university life that cannot be documented totally from data amassed by national data collection institutions, such as the attitudes, social and economic background, and welfare of minority college students. We also take a look at the kinds of programs that minority college students are enrolled in and the amount and kind of assistance these students are getting from colleges, state governments, and the federal government. In short, while we would like to stick as close as possible to inferences from available data in drawing conclusions, we will examine areas considered crucial to students in their matriculation through institutions of higher education.

The major racial and ethnic groups in the United States will be examined relevant to the majority population. The major groups examined are Native Americans (American Indians), blacks, Asian Americans, Hispanic Americans, and subgroups of the major groups. Our information allowed us in certain instances to look at subgroups such as the Native American population by major tribal groupings;

1

the Asian American subgroups--Chinese, Japanese, and Filipinos; and the Hispanic American subgroups--Puerto Ricans, Cubans, and Mexicans.

Because we are using data gathered by national data collection organizations, definitions for each of the racial and ethnic groupings are those defined by the data collection agencies. The U.S. Bureau of the Census 1970 survey allowed individuals completing the Census questionnaire to define themselves in terms of racial or ethnic identity. Other data collection sources, such as the American Council on Education (ACE) and the Office for Civil Rights (OCR) within the Department of Health, Education and Welfare, allowed the institutions in which students were enrolled to define their student population in terms of race and ethnic identification. The Current Population Reports (CPR) published annually by the Census Bureau uses yet another technique of identifying college students by race and ethnicity: the perceptions of the interviewers in identifying the racial and ethnic origin of the people being interviewed. Basically, one would have to conclude that in a majority of instances, except for Current Population Reports, individuals in question provide their own racial and ethnic identification. While it is true that OCR and the ACE get their data from institutions, it is a common practice among institutions of higher education in collecting their data to ask students during registration to identify themselves by race and/or ethnicity. Therefore, it seems like a fair conclusion to state that while institutions provide these agencies with data, origin of these data come from the individuals themselves.

Needless to say, categories of race and ethnicity are not mutually exclusive. For example, a Hispanic American may be also identified as white, Native American, Asian, or black. A Native American from mixed ethnic or racial background may elect to classify himself as Native American, white, Hispanic American, Asian, or black. While these data are not necessarily "clean," they do provide us with each individual's major reference group. That is, each individual in the United States is asked to make a choice, to select the group that he identifies with the most. In this sense one would have to conclude that these data are fairly accurate as to minority group membership.

ORGANIZATION OF THE BOOK

To do the analysis that we have mentioned we have organized the book in the following manner. In Chapter 1 the background and a description of the intent of the book are given. Major data sources are presented as well as an explanation of their strong points and their limitations. The content of each of the major areas of the text is described, along with a brief history of minorities enrolled in institutional higher education in the United States.

What are the benefits that minority group individuals may expect to get from higher education? Or, put another way, why is it necessary for minority-group members to attend institutions of higher education in representative numbers and percentages? What are the economic, social, and psychological benefits to be derived by individuals attending institutions of higher education; or, what are the negative ramifications for groups who are not adequately represented in institutions of higher education? In Chapter 2 situations are presented in an attempt to show that it is imperative in a modern technological society that minority-group members be adequately represented in institutions of higher education. It is argued that to be equal or to gain a measure of parity in this society individual members from the various minority groups must gain a fair share of postsecondary education. From an individual point of view, benefits derived from a college education are unmistakably clear. From a group perspective a college education is also important. Since racism is still prevalent in this country, this leads us to the conclusion that a college education is beneficial to the individual minority member and to the minority group to which he or she belongs. One may further conclude that one index of group equality in this country is their attendance at institutions of higher education. We must say, however, that this is only one measure of equality in this country because there are minority groups who have, in the past, achieved a high level of participation in higher education (namely Chinese, Japanese, and Cuban Americans) and they have not achieved parity with whites in an economic, social, and psychological sense.

Therefore, Chapter 2 explores and examines the benefits to be derived from the completion of a college education by members of minority groups. First, the relationship between educational attainment and earned income is examined; and it is concluded that regardless of the racial and ethnic group concerned there is a positive correlation between one's level of educational attainment and one's earned income. In addition, there is a discussion of who attends college. It was hypothesized that individuals who attend college will be the ruling elites of the future and as such will hold powerful and status positions in the community. The converse to this hypothesis states that individuals not completing a college education should not expect membership in the ruling elite and should not expect to occupy powerful and status positions in the country. Evidence is overwhelming that only individuals who have matriculated successfully through an institution of higher education will occupy status positions in this country today and only those individuals are likely to occupy such

positions in the future. Therefore, if we combine the economic benefits of education with the social benefits of occupying status positions,
the achievement of these two ends will produce positive gratifying
psychological effects for individuals. It has always been psychologically advantageous for an individual to be on top of the heap.

Chapter 3, the heart of the text, deals with minority enrollment in colleges and universities in the United States. The first
part of the chapter deals with undergraduate enrollment for the four
major minority groups. Data are presented from a variety of sources
specifying the number and percentage of minority students enrolled
in various colleges and universities in the United States. These data
are also separated by the level of offering within institutions of higher
education, namely, two-year colleges, four-year colleges, and universities. Data are also separated by level of control--public or
private. These data were gathered from a variety of national data
collection sources, thereby reducing the margin of error and allow-
ing us to make definitive predictions and projections regarding the
need for increased efforts to enroll more minorities in institutions
of higher education.

Chapter 4 measures the productivity of U.S. colleges and universities in terms of earned degrees granted to minority college students. An earned degree is perhaps not the only measure of college
and university productivity but in a society that values credentials it
is the most definitive measure of productivity. We assume that students who matriculate in an institution of higher education profited
from that experience; but only if the student completes the college
program and is granted the degree is he considered a final product
of the institution. The estimation of the number of minorities that
earned degrees from undergraduate schools was computed by figures
based on the percentage of minority students in the upper division of
undergraduate schools. This weighing of the earned degree population was based upon the assumption that the percentage of minorities
who reach the upper divisional level is probably a more precise indi-
cator of who finally finishes college than the gross percentage that
involves freshmen and sophomores. Information on graduate degrees
granted are combined with graduate enrollment figures in Chapter 6.

Chapter 5 discusses mainly minority enrollment in engineering
and pharmacy schools at both the undergraduate and graduate level.
Earned degrees for engineering and pharmacy as well as earned doctoral degrees for the sciences and mathematics are also given.

Chapter 6 deals exclusively with the graduate and professional
schools such as law, medicine, and dentistry, and doctoral degrees
outside of law, medicine, and dentistry. Our graduate and professional school data are accurate; however, they are not as extensive
in scope and content as those for the undergraduate enrollment.

First, except for the professional schools such as law, dentistry, and medicine, few statistics are kept for the other disciplines regarding minority student enrollment. Data in the other disciplines are generally lumped together simply as graduate minority student enrollment. It is rather difficult to specify the exact number of minority students enrolled in biochemistry or history. Second, attendance in graduate studies is not always an indication of how well or poorly minority students are progressing in those programs. Full-time graduate study status may not indicate an advantage over a student who is signed up with a part-time study. In fact, a student who is enrolled for part-time graduate studies may be engaged in more advanced-level work and with greater productivity than a student who is registered for full-time credit. It is often a common practice within graduate schools to allow students who are working on their dissertations to sign up for just a few credit hours to remain registered with the university (which is a requirement). Relatively speaking, our graduate school data are not as comprehensive as our undergraduate data; but given the scope and nature of graduate education these data are still essential for a comprehensive look at minorities in higher education.

An in-depth view of the status of minority college enrollment in five large urban states—California, Florida, Illinois, New York, and Texas—is taken in Chapter 7. The usual practice of lumping data together for a national picture does not allow for the necessary examination of minorities in our culturally pluralistic population that a close-up view of five states would. At least one large metropolitan area is examined within each of the states.

Chapter 8, first section, deals with economic indicators and the minority college student. There is a discussion of the possible sources of the minority student's income and ability to handle college costs. Economic indicators regarding the minority college student's family background are examined as we attempt to assess implications of his economic strength or lack of strength for college attendance and graduation. Available data from a number of sources are presented in order to indicate the economic strength of the minority student's family and his community. After reviewing data on the economic status of the minority student we concluded that it is essential that he receive support from sources outside the family to attend college. The exact kind and scope of that need is explained and discussed in more detail in Chapters 9 and 10.

The second section of Chapter 8 is an extension of the first section but it deals more with the social characteristics of the minority college student and his family. The precollege preparation of the minority college student is discussed within the parameters of the kind and quality of education received. Data are also presented as

to the number and percentage of minority students who graduate from
high school and the percentage of minority students who are in the
college-age category. There is no question that minority students
from socially disadvantaged backgrounds can successfully matriculate
through college. For more than 100 years minority students from
disadvantaged backgrounds have entered and matriculated successfully through the most prestigious colleges and universities in this
country and abroad.

This chapter discusses affirmative action programs designed
to recruit and fund minority student attendance on college and university campuses. Affirmative action in this case is defined as efforts
by institutions of higher education to be aggressive in the selection
and recruitment of minority students for undergraduate and graduate
schools. The various kinds and types of "equal opportunity programs"
operating at the various college and university campuses around the
country are discussed. We find that many economically and educationally disadvantaged students are matriculating at institutions of
higher education only because of the affirmative action efforts. We
conclude that unless these affirmative action efforts are continued
the number of minority students on campuses throughout the country
will decline.

Chapter 8 also discusses the various kinds of student financial
aid programs sponsored by the federal government. The various
programs aimed specifically at the Native American population,
through the Bureau of Indian Affairs, are briefly described. Chapter
9 examines the college campus life of minority students. Special attention is given to the two largest minority groups: blacks and Hispanic Americans. We also compare the campus life of minorities
at two- and four-year colleges.

Chapter 10 discusses the future of minorities in higher education and makes projections about the status of minority higher education in the immediate future based upon enrollment figures, social
and economic factors affecting minority college students, affirmative
action programs sponsored by the federal government and state and
local agencies, and the financial aid packages that are now available
to minority students from the federal government. The major conclusion reached in this chapter is that during the next decade the enrollment of minority students in institutions of higher education will
be stabilized at the current level. Factors contributing to this decline in the rate of increase are the social and political climate within
the country, economic factors affecting the ability of government to
fund students in institutions of higher education, the increased cost of
attending school, and a continuous deterioration of precollege education provided to minority youngsters in our large urban and metropolitan school districts. All of these factors have combined to halt

the continued rate of increase in minority student college enrollment. Specific policy recommendations to improve minority college enrollment are outlined.

METHODOLOGY AND DATA ANALYSIS

In trying to present a clear and comprehensive picture of
minority status in higher education, a number of considerations
guided the selection of data sources, as well as the presentation of
data. The first consideration was to collect data that would be
reasonably comprehensive. There are many sources of information
concerning minority groups in higher education, but in many cases
methods of data collection and classification are different, so that
comparisons over a period of time are difficult. Consequently, a
decision was made to rely primarily on national data sources. Publications of national data are usually at least two years old when released.

The second concern was to establish certain target years
(1968-74) so that estimates could be made of changes in the course
of time. The choice of target years was dictated by the availability
of data. The dates were dictated by the availability of the Office for
Civil Rights survey and Census Bureau reports.

To provide a framework for interpreting data on enrollment,
background information on the characteristics of the U.S. population
was deemed necessary. This information is presented on a national
basis and for each of the states selected for special consideration.

Definition of Terms

Level of offering. The extent of academic offerings by year
and program type. Three levels are reviewed in this study: two-
year colleges, four-year colleges, and universities: (1) two-year
colleges are institutions that offer less than four years of college
work but beyond the high-school level; (2) four-year colleges are institutions that offer at least a bachelor's degree but less than a doctorate; (3) universities are institutions that offer doctoral-level programs; (4) four-year institutions are a combination of four-year
colleges and universities.

Full-time students. There are two definitions for full-time
students. The Office for Civil Rights study defines full-time status
as a student enrolled with 75 percent of what the institution considers the required load for a full-time student. The second definition
involves data from the U.S. Office of Education. Information from

this survey uses each institution's definition of full-time status, which differs from one institution to another. Credit hours for full-time undergraduate status generally differs from graduate status.

Underrepresentation. This term indicates comparative data of college enrollment or attainment to that of the general population for a specific racial or ethnic group. For example, to indicate black undergraduate representation a comparison would be made between those currently enrolled and those who might theoretically be enrolled, given their representation in the population. If in 1974 the black population were 11.4 percent, one would expect that the full-time black undergraduate enrollment would be 1,165,505 (11.4 percent of the total 10,223,729). The actual count, however, is 921,218 or 9.0 percent. Therefore, black representation is only 79 percent of what it should be.

Full-time equivalent (FTE). This term refers to the cumulative number of credit hours taken by students, divided by the number of hours considered minimum requirement for a full-time student. This is not a head or body count. For example, 100 full-time equivalent students may involve 200 students who take an assorted number of credit hours. Generally, the number of FTEs ranges somewhere between the number of full-time students and the combined number of full-time and part-time students.

Lower division. Students enrolled in their first and second years of college study.

Upper division. Students enrolled in their third and fourth years of study.

Resident undergraduates. Students enrolled in degree credit undergraduate programs, exclusive of extension courses.

Socioeconomic status (SES). This term, as used in this study, refers to income received or earned by individuals or groups in a specific time interval. While current income is somewhat inadequate as a measure of a person's status in life, it is used here because it is the only measure of SES on a national sampling of individuals and groups. Inferences generated by using current income to define SES should be viewed with caution.

Standard Metropolitan Statistical Area (SMSA). This is a notation used by the U.S. Census to refer to major cities and their adjacent surroundings.

Major Data Sources

Office for Civil Rights data (OCR). These data were submitted to OCR by institutions via questionnaires. The institutions defined their student population by various racial and ethnic groups.

(1) <u>Strengths of the data</u>: This represents the only head count of college students by race and ethnicity. It is a national study that uses the same questionnaire for each institution. (2) <u>Weaknesses of the data</u>: The institutions were allowed to define the racial and ethnic composition of their student population. Information on blacks and Asian Americans fared favorably with other data sources (Census Bureau and American Council on Education), but was less favorable for Hispanic Americans. However, the worst correlation appeared for Native Americans. This trend was consistent for all states that were sampled. In some states there were more Native Americans enrolled in college than listed in the college-age group by the U.S. Census. Therefore, the statistics on Native Americans are of questionable reliability

U.S. Office of Education data. These data involve information on enrollment without racial breakdowns, but percentages computed from the OCR data were used to compute racial enrollment figures. As indicated earlier, information on Native Americans is probably less valid than for others. These data used a different definition of a full-time student.

U.S. Census data. The census data used a 15 percent or 5 percent sample of the "sample" population (60 percent of the total) to compute estimates of educational attainment or enrollment. The Census data are weighted toward urban areas and therefore might be less valid for nonurban dwellers such as Native Americans and Hispanic Americans. (1) <u>Strengths of the data</u>. These are national in scope and contain longitudinal information which is readily available. (2) <u>Weaknesses of the data</u>. A very small "sample" was used to estimate enrollment and it was weighted toward urban areas and against disadvantaged communities. For example: (a) <u>Puerto Ricans</u>. In 1960 the Census did not collect data outside the five southwestern states (Arizona, California, Colorado, New Mexico, and Texas). In 1970 it collected information only in New York, New Jersey, and Pennsylvania. The Census Bureau did not differentiate between those individuals who listed themselves as both white and Puerto Rican or "part" Puerto Rican. The definition of race was not clear. Only 5 percent of the Puerto Ricans who were surveyed listed themselves as both Puerto Rican and black. Therefore it can be assumed that the overlap is larger between individuals who listed themselves as both white and Puerto Rican. (b) <u>Mexican Americans</u>. In 1960 and 1970 only the five southwestern states listed above were surveyed for people of Mexican American origin (Spanish surnamed or persons of Mexican American origin). No provisions were made for "part" Spanish surnamed or those who might list themselves as both white and Spanish surnamed, or both Spanish surnamed and Native Americans. (c) <u>Spanish surnamed or of Spanish origin</u>. Survey asked for

individuals of Spanish origin outside the five southwestern states
and three northeastern states. (d) Orientals. In this book the term
Asian Americans is preferred. This is a survey of information on
Japanese, Chinese, and Filipino Americans, 1960 and 1970. However, the 1970 data exclude some 92,000 Hawaiians who considered
themselves "mixed" or part Hawaiian. Therefore, the 1960 data
are not comparable to the 1970 data. (e) Blacks. In 1960 full or
complete information on blacks was fused under the heading of "non-
whites," including Asian Americans. However, detailed information
was collected for New York, Texas, California, Illinois, South Carolina, and Michigan. In 1970 information on blacks in all states was
collected. The accuracy of Census data on blacks between the ages
of 15 and 24 is questionable. Blacks in this age group are 16 percentage points less than the 5-to-14 age group. For whites the percentage spread is only 3 percent. It must be concluded that young
blacks were missed by the Census takers. Accordingly, the Census
data must be viewed as a good first approximation; but those who desire more definitive information will have to produce more comprehensive data.

A crucial problem of the Census data involves a head count of
ethnic-group members who consider themselves both ethnic-group
members and white. As a result, the sum total of all subgroups
within some states exceeds the total population of the state. It is im-
possible to compute or estimate the amount and degree of overlap.
The method employed in this study was to compute the ethnic and
racial groups and subtract this number from the states' total population, then define that number as the white population (whites who
are considered neither Spanish-surnamed Americans, "mixed,"
Native Americans, nor Puerto Ricans). While there may be flaws
in this method of computing ethnic-group membership percentages,
it is the best technique for producing mutually exclusive categories.

The Census Bureau's Current Population Reports conduct an
annual survey of the population, which are not always compatible
with the data provided by the decennial census of the population.
Further, information from a CPR in one year may not be compatible
for information on the same topic collected for another year. For
example, the data collected from March 1973 through March 1975
by Current Population Surveys are not entirely comparable to earlier
years because of the revisions in the Current Population Survey.
The major item affecting compatibility at the overall national level
is the introduction to population controls based on the 1970 Census.
Figures for previous years, except where noted, tied in with 1960
Census base-population controls. Basically, these changes should
have no substantial impact on summary measures (such as medians,
means, and percent distributions).

Data collected for the current population survey from August 1972 to the present were based on a sample spread over the 50 states and the District of Columbia. While approximately 47,000 occupied households are eligible for interviews each month, only about 2,000 are visited and interviewed. Data from these interviews are then utilized to estimate the population as a whole. The estimating procedure used in the current population survey involves the inflation of the weighted sample results to independent estimates of the civilian noninstitutional population of the United States by age, race, and sex. These independent estimates are based on statistics from the previous decennial survey of the population, statistics of birth, death, immigration, and statistics on the strength of the armed forces. A major source of error with the current population survey is the noninclusion of the individuals confined in institutions such as prisons, mental institutions, and the armed forces. The noninclusion of institutional data may bias the Current Population Survey against a true estimate of minority population measures. It is a known fact that minorities such as blacks, Native Americans, and Hispanic Americans are overrepresented in prisons and the armed forces. Therefore, an estimation of the minority population without including members of the armed forces and people who have been institutionalized in prisons will further bias the data against the minority male population since most members of the armed forces and prisons are male. While this bias may exist, it is not considered to be one of major proportion and should leave the data produced by the Current Population Survey fairly accurate for gross estimates. It is expected, with statistical estimates such as the current population survey, that a small standard error will exist. Another weakness of the CPR is that they tend to do special reports only on black and Hispanic American populations.

SUMMARY

We hope that the goals set forth—to present current data on minority representation in institutions of higher education—have been achieved in the next nine chapters. In addition to our major goal on representation we have attempted to highlight several subgoals: the selectivity of institutions attended by minority students, the benefits to be derived from a college education, the financial capability of education, and affirmative action by local, state, and federal governments to aid the economically and educationally disadvantaged students in their pursuit of a college education.

Finally, we argue that an opportunity to attend college should not be hampered solely by the financial resources of a student's family. Up until 1970 college attendance by a qualified applicant rested mainly upon his ability to secure funds from financially resourceful (and willing) parents. We argue that a person's financial position due to an accident of birth should not prevent him from attending college. To correct this grave social injustice, in which minorities share the greatest burden, we have offered specific recommendations in Chapter 10. Minimally, it is hoped that these recommendations will initiate a national debate on the issues reviewed in the text and maximally that these recommendations will serve as a guide for corrective legislation by local, state, and federal governments.

2

THE BENEFITS OF
A COLLEGE EDUCATION

The benefits to be derived from a college education can best be described by answering three questions. First, why do people attend college? Second, who attends college? Third, what is the probability that every qualified college-age person who wants to will have an opportunity to pursue a college education? The questions posed may be viewed from an individualistic point of view or from a racial or ethnic-group-membership point of view. The mode of analysis used here will be mainly from a group-membership perspective. The rationale for this analysis is based upon the assumption that racism in the United States is highly correlated with an individual's group-membership identity.

WHY ATTEND COLLEGE?

By virtue of the vast resources allocated to an institution of higher education to train highly skilled persons, this society (through its government and private universities) has established a high priority for the production of a pool of college-educated individuals; and our reward structure grants such trained individuals a high-status position and income commensurate with that position. This position will place college-trained individuals above the masses in terms of personal prestige and gratification by being a member of the ruling elite. If one can justifiably use the term elite to refer to those individuals in our society who occupy status positions (Taubman and Wales 1974), then it seems fair to assume that more than 90 percent of all individuals occupying status positions in this country will have attended and/or graduated from an institution of higher education. This analysis may not hold true for all societies

but in the United States it is more than a truism, it is an accomplished fact. Data on earned income and educational attainment indicate a higher correlation between educational attainment and median
income: A male with four years of college education is expected to
have an earned income 316.4 percent greater than a male with less
than eight years of education; likewise a female with four years of
college education is expected to earn 303.8 percent more than a
female with less than an eighth-grade education (see Tables 2.1 and
2.2). This is true even if one compares individuals within a racial
group.

TABLE 2.1

Education and Income in the United States,
March 1974, Median Income.
(in dollars)

	Men	Percent of Base ($4,551)	Women	Percent of Base ($2,132)
Elementary school				
Less than 8 years	4,551	100.0	2,132	100.0
8 years	6,621	145.5	2,417	113.4
High school				
1-3 years	9,017	198.1	3,210	150.6
4 years	11,290	248.1	4,209	197.4
College				
1-3 years	12,322	270.0	4,912	230.4
4 years	14,401	316.4	6,477	303.8
5 years or more	16,162	355.1	9,182	430.7

Source: The Chronicle of Higher Education--Fact-File, from
U.S., Bureau of the Census, March 22, 1976.

        Data on black earned income and educational attainment also
confirms the fact that even though the black educated individual may
not earn as much as the similarly educated white individual, the
black educated person stands a greater chance of earning more than
the less-educated black. Evidence is clear that the minority person
who desires to increase his earning power must seek to maximize
his educational attainment. Even though there may be variations

TABLE 2.2

Income of Males and Schooling, 1970

Earnings (in dollars) and Median Years of Schooling

	999 or Less	1,000– 2,999	3,000– 3,999	4,000– 5,999	5,000– 6,999	7,000– 9,999	10,000– 14,999	15,000– 24,999	25,000 and Over
U.S. total	8.3	8.5	9.0	10.0	11.3	12.2	12.6	14.4	16.2
Blacks	6.4	7.0	8.5	9.3	10.5	11.6	12.4	13.7	13.6
Black ratio	.77	.82	.94	.93	.93	.95	.98	.95	.84

Education Completed and Median Income (in dollars) Earned

	Elementary School			High School		College				
	1-3 Years	5-7 Years	8 Years	1-3 Years	4 Years	1-2 Years	3 Years	4 Years	5 Years	6 Years
U.S. total	3,658	5,000	6,030	7,564	9,042	10,446	11,233	14,229	13,092	17,879
Blacks	3,018	4,064	4,669	5,351	6,295	6,992	7,163	8,218	9,338	12,888
Black ratio	.83	.81	.77	.71	.70	.67	.64	.58	.71	.72

Source: U.S. Bureau of the Census, Subject Reports, Educational Attainment, PC (2)-5 B, March 1973.

between the different racial and ethnic groups in terms of economic earning power, given a certain amount of education, it is still true that for a particular individual, regardless of racial or ethnic identification, who desires to increase his income or status in life he must seek to maximize his education.

WHO ATTENDS COLLEGE?

The second question posed was who attends college? In 1974 10,223,729 individuals were enrolled in institutions of higher education in the United States. However, when one attempts to categorize this enrollment in terms of racial and ethnic identification, it is clear that representation is not equal (see Table 2.3). All various minority groups, in general, are underrepresented by about 50 percent in institutions of higher education: blacks 40 percent, and Hispanic Americans about 80 percent. The Asian American college population indicated an overrepresentation of 10 percent in relation to the general population; however, Asian Americans are underrepresented when compared to the percentage of Asian Americans who have graduated from high school in relation to their college enrollment. While the country as a whole has a high school graduation rate of 52.3 percent, the Asian American rates are 68.8 percent for Japanese Americans, 57.8 percent for Chinese Americans, 54.7 percent for Filipino Americans, and 53.2 percent for the Hawaiian population. It is demonstrably clear that the Asian American college-age population is underrepresented in view of the higher-than-average high school graduation rate.

On the other hand, it is not simply a matter of percentages and number of individuals attending college, it is also a matter of what types of colleges students attend. We find that in the status hierarchy of higher education beginning with two-year colleges, four-year colleges, and the universities, respectively, the two-year college is at the bottom of the hierarchy (Hansen et al. 1972). Even though we have a large number of minorities enrolled in institutions of higher education, there is a disproportionate number of minorities enrolled in the less-prestigious colleges and universities (Karabel 1972). For example, we find that blacks, Native Americans, and Hispanic Americans are overrepresented in two-year and four-year colleges, but are decisively underrepresented in prestigious universities. Graduates from the prestigious research-type universities have advantages over graduates from less-prestigious colleges: They are more likely to have first crack at status positions within business and industry, first choice as faculty members with prestigious universities, and first choice as government officials. Therefore, even

TABLE 2.3

School Enrollment and Educational Attainment of the
U.S. Population by Race, 1970

	Population	Percent High School Graduates 25 Years Old and Over	Median Age	Median School Completed 25 Years Old and Over	College Enrollment 3–34 Years Old	Completed College 25 Years Old and Over
White	169,089,254	57.1	27.7	12.2	6,393,230	8,527,633
Black	22,549,815	31.4	22.3	9.8	430,747	455,959
American Indian	763,594	33.3	20.4	9.8	14,191	12,195
Japanese	588,324	68.8	31.8	12.5	38,329	56,323
Chinese	431,583	57.8	26.8	12.4	51,526	58,241
Filipino	336,731	54.7	26.2	12.2	12,738	39,751
Hawaiian population	99,958	53.2		12.1	2,830	2,518
Spanish origin	9,072,602	32.1	21.1	9.1	155,497	179,106
Spanish surname (southwestern states)	4,667,975	28.7	20.2	8.6	94,368	65,292
Puerto Ricans	1,391,463	22.1	20.3	8.6	17,705	12,914
Mexican origin	4,532,435	24.2	19.3	8.1	73,376	44,741
Cuban origin	544,600	43.9	31.7	10.3	12,903	35,513
Total	203,210,158	52.3	29.5	12.1	6,966,033	11,697,672

Sources: U.S. Bureau of the Census, Subject Reports, and Characteristics of the Population, 1973.

17

though we have an increase in the number and percentage of minorities enrolled and graduating from college, they are still less
competitive in the market place, because on the average the less-
prestigious institutions are attended by minority groups.

WHAT ARE THE OPPORTUNITIES
TO ATTEND COLLEGE?

The third question posed was what is the probability that every
qualified college-aged person who wants to attend college will have
an opportunity to do so? This question makes it very tempting to
discuss the views of those who have stated that there is no correlation between upward mobility and education. But we feel that whether
that statement is true or false, it has little bearing on the proposition
that every U.S. citizen ought to have his rights protected equally
under the laws as stated in the Fourteenth Amendment to the Con-
stitution. If there is no relationship between education attainment
and upward mobility, we feel that minorities ought to have an equal
chance to be equally disappointed by the negative benefits to be derived from a college education (Wright 1972). However, such an
assumption seems totally ridiculous in light of the resources allocated to train college-educated people and society's reward structure that is designed to motivate people to pursue a college education.
That reward structure is so totally ingrained into the whole social,
political, and economic fiber of this country that it is mandatory for
anyone who desires to be a top businessman, a top government offi-
cial, a top politician, or a top anything (see Table 2.4).

While we have discussed the economic and social benefits derived from a college education, we find that the combination of
achieving these two measures will make for a much happier person,
psychologically. It is difficult to believe that an individual who
occupies a position at the top of his profession and who commands
top salary is less happy than the person at the bottom of that profession with a minimum salary. The question begs little discussion
because if this assumption were not true, society's reward structure (of motivation) that drives individuals to pursue lengthy years
of college education would not work. Therefore, the assumption is
made that people strive to achieve things in life because, in fact,
they assume or they know that they will be happier after they have
achieved the ends sought.

For a minority-group individual to look around and not see
members of his ethnic or racial group among individuals who occupy
status and decision-making positions in the community is in itself
psychologically harmful. For the minority child it is a healthy sight

TABLE 2.4

Occupation of Employed Persons by Race, 1970,
50 States and District of Columbia

Number and Percent of Population

Profession	Whites 83.7%	Blacks 11.1%	Hispanic Americans 4.6%
Dentists	84,605	1,983	1,164
	96.3	2.3	1.3
Engineers	1,260,122	18,596	28,334
	96.8	1.4	2.2
Lawyers and judges	255,812	3,236	3,783
	98.4	1.2	1.4
Life and physical scientists	192,929	6,392	4,711
	93.9	3.1	2.3
Physicians	240,409	5,084	9,362
	94.0	2.0	3.7
Teachers	4,083,372	304,930	92,662
	91.5	6.0	2.0

Source: U.S. Bureau of the Census, Census of the Population, 1970.

19

to see members of his group participating actively in all aspects of community life. In short, this society demands a college education for those who wish a greater share in the prestige and resources of this country; minorities must get past the gatekeeper--our colleges and universities; and if they are successful in getting past the gate-keeper, chances are they will be so rewarded and thus achieve the economic, social, and psychological gratification that goes with that achievement.

3

NATIVE AMERICANS

In 1970 there were 792,730 Native Americans residing in the United States. The 1970 population figures represent a 51.4 percent increase over the 1960 population; the 1960 population is a 46.5 percent increase over the 1950 population; the 1950 population is 3.5 percent more than the 1940 population; and the 1940 population is only 0.6 percent larger than the 1930 population (see Table 3.1). These uneven changes in the estimated population of Native Americans suggest that either the Census takers were not very competent in doing their job or that more and more Native Americans are willing to identify themselves as such. It seems unlikely that the 51.4 percent increase in the 1970 population over the 1960 population is due mainly to new individuals being born, but it may be due more to the counting of individuals in 1970 who were not counted in 1960. We are citing these figures just to indicate to the reader that there is some unreliability in the actual head count of Native Americans. We also feel that the actual number is perhaps somewhat larger than that reported by the Bureau of the Census.

Native Americans resided in what is now the United States of America thousands of years before the arrival of the white man from Europe. Native Americans also preceded the arrival of black Americans from Africa as slaves, the arrival of Asian Americans from Asia and the Pacific, as well as the arrival of Hispanic Americans from South America and the Caribbean islands.

Despite their long history and tenure in the United States, published literature on the history of Native American education is very sparse. It might be of interest to note that the charters of America's first colleges and universities (Harvard, Princeton, William and

Mary, and Dartmouth, for example) stipulated that their mission was to educate white and Indian boys. However, few Indian children have ever attended or graduated from these institutions.

TABLE 3.1

Native American Population of the United States, 1900 to 1970

Census Year	Native American Population	Change from Preceding Census	
		Number	Percent
1970	792,730	269,139	51.4
1960	523,591	166,092	47.5
1950	357,499	12,247	3.5
1940	345,252	1,900	0.6
1930	343,352	98,915	40.5
1920	244,437	-32,490	-11.7
1910	276,927	39,731	16.8
1900	237,196	--	--

Note: Changes in the growth of the Native American population resulted in part from differences in procedures for classifying persons of mixed racial descent. Minus sign (-) denotes decrease.

Source: U.S. Bureau of the Census, Subject Reports, American Indians in the U.S., PC (2) - IF, June 1973, Table II.

At various times, Native Americans have been educated in Christian missionary schools, federal schools, and state and local public schools. However, there were exceptions: the Choctaw Indians operated their own schools from about 1825 until 1842 (Henry 1972); and the State of North Carolina provided segregated schooling for the children of the more than 30,000 Lumbee Indians of Robeson County, North Carolina. The educational history of the Lumbee Indians is unique in that they have never lived on a reservation nor have they received the services and support of the Bureau of Indian Affairs.

As colonial American settlers spread across the countryside westward, Eastern and Midwestern tribes were forced to give up their land for unsettled areas in the West. What followed was a long period of concentration on reservations which limited Native Americans to small segments of land area. Native Americans, forced

from their Eastern homes, had to adapt to new ecological surroundings. It should be noted that Native Americans are composed of a
wide variety of cultural backgrounds and historical experiences,
and they speak two hundred or more languages and sublanguages.

In 1928 a government report known as the Merian Report (1928)
documented the poor living conditions on Indian reservations. The
report revealed shocking poverty, ill health, poor education, and
widespread deprivation on the reservations. The report was basically
responsible for the Indian Reorganization Act of 1934. This act called
for involvement of Native American leadership in decision making
about their lives. What followed was a period of positive attitude
toward Indian life and culture by the government. However, in 1951
a reversal of positive government policy toward Native Americans
developed which resulted in a call to curtail the Bureau of Indian Affairs (BIA) activities and eventually terminating protection to Native
Americans on reservations. Under this policy economic and political developments within Native American communities was severely
retarded. In 1961, however, there was the beginning of a new approach by the federal government which called for a resumption of
services provided by the BIA.

Native American education, in general, is distinct from that
of any other group. Because it is so different, at the elementary
and secondary level, from that for all other citizens, we feel that it
deserves special attention. Unlike other groups or individuals in
this country, whites included, the education of Native American children is a legal responsibility of the federal government. This responsibility, however, is limited to the children of Native Americans
who live on reservations or who come under responsibility of the BIA.
For all other citizens the responsibility for elementary and secondary
education is a local and state responsibility, not a federal responsibility.

About 52,908 Native American children in 1974 were enrolled
in schools operated or funded by the BIA. This represented a 4.1
percent drop in the number of children enrolled in BIA schools from
1973. In that same year, 49,524 students attended schools operated
by the BIA; 32,454 attended BIA Boarding Schools; 17,068 attended
BIA-operated day schools; while 3,384 lived in federal dormitories
supported by the BIA and attended local public schools (not operated
by the BIA) (see Tables 3.2 and 3.3). While there was generally a
slight decline in each category of schooling operated or funded by the
BIA for Indian children in 1974, compared to 1973, the biggest decline (14.4 percent) was reported in the number of students living in
federal dormitories. Also in 1974 approximately 1,566 Indian children graduated from BIA-operated high schools, 2,631 completed
eighth grade education, and 357 completed some form of postsecondary
education (see Table 3.4). The largest group of Indian schools are
Navajo, 20,596; followed by Aberdeen, 9,412; and Juneau, 5,823.

TABLE 3.2

Enrollment (all ages) by Types of Schools Operated by the Bureau
of Indian Affairs, Fiscal Years 1973 and 1974

Area	Total Enrollment		Boarding Enrollment		Day Enrollment	
	1973	1974	1973	1974	1973	1974
Aberdeen	9,412	8,797	3,958	3,727	5,396	5,252
Albuquerque	3,850	3,765	1,830	1,862	1,834	1,903
Anadarko	2,634	2,428	2,634	2,428	--	--
Cherokee	1,291	1,253	--	--	--	1,253
Choctaw	1,446	1,383	1,132	1,068	314	315
Juneau	5,823	5,866	568	664	5,255	5,202
Muskogee	684	616	684	618	--	--
Navajo	20,596	19,860	19,331	18,605	1,265	1,255
Phoenix	4,765	4,779	2,888	2,934	1,877	1,845
Portland	647	550	647	550	--	--
Seminole	32	43	--	--	32	43
Total	51,180*	49,524	33,672	32,456	17,264	17,068

*Federal facilities were provided for a total of 55,051 children, 3,871 of whom lived in federal dormitories and attended public schools fiscal year 1973; 1974 fiscal year there were 52,908 children, 3,384 of whom lived in dormitories and attended public schools.

Source: U.S. Department of the Interior, Bureau of Indian Affairs, Office of Indian Education Programs, Fiscal Year 1973 Statistics Concerning Indian Education and Fiscal Year 1974 Statistics Concerning Indian Education (Washington, D.C.: U.S. Government Printing Office, 1974, 1975).

TABLE 3.3

Enrollment in Schools Operated and Funded by the Bureau
of Indian Affairs, Fiscal Years 1973 and 1974

	1973[a]	1974[b]	Percent Change
Total, all schools	55,051	52,908	-4.1
Total, BIA schools	51,180	49,524	-3.3
Boarding schools	33,672	32,456	-3.7
Day schools	17,264	17,068	-1.1
Hospital programs	244	--	--
Live in dormitories, attend public schools	3,871	3,384	-14.4

[a]In 1973 BIA provided education for 55,051 children; 51,180 attended schools operated by BIA, while 3,871 lived in 19 federal dormitories and attended public schools.

[b]In 1974 BIA provided education for 52,908 children; 49,524 attended schools operated by BIA, while 3,384 lived in 19 federal dormitories and attended public schools.

Source: U.S. Department of the Interior, Bureau of Indian Affairs, Office of Indian Education Programs, Fiscal Year 1973 Statistics Concerning Indian Education and Fiscal Year 1974 Statistics Concerning Indian Education (Washington, D.C.: U.S. Government Printing Office, 1974, 1975).

TABLE 3.4

Completions and Number of Graduates of Schools Operated by the
Bureau of Indian Affairs, Fiscal Year 1974

Area	High School Graduates	8th Grade Completions	Postgraduate Completions or Placements
Aberdeen	279	531	--
Albuquerque	116	47	138
Anadarko	158	60	195
Cherokee*	33	94	--
Choctaw*	37	92	--
Juneau	79	435	--
Muskogee	52	42	--
Navajo	442	1,073	24
Phoenix	250	257	--
Portland	120	--	--
Seminole*	--	--	--
Total	1,566	2,631	357

*Under jurisdiction of Eastern Area office headquartered in Washington, D.C.

Source: U.S. Department of the Interior, Bureau of Indian Affairs, Office of Indian Education Programs, Fiscal Year 1974 Statistics Concerning Indian Education (Washington, D.C.: U.S. Government Printing Office, 1975).

Data on Native American college enrollments are sometimes conflicting and confusing. First, data from the BIA are not helpful in estimating the total Native American college enrollment; their data only record the enrollment of those Indians who come under the auspices of the BIA. A 1974 estimate of the undergraduate college enrollment of Native Americans by the Office for Civil Rights indicates that there are 59,394 Native Americans enrolled in institutions of higher education, which represents 0.6 percent of the total college-age population (see Table 3.5). However, a 1974 survey by the American Council on Education indicates that for the same year 0.9 percent of all entering freshmen were Native Americans. These data would suggest at first sight that Native Americans are slightly overrepresented in higher education based upon their percentage in the population, 0.4 percent.

TABLE 3.5

Native American Undergraduate Enrollment, Summary Data

	Total, U.S.	Percent of College Population	Percent of Freshmen Who Are Native American	Number Enrolled in Bureau of Indian Affairs Programs
1966	--	--	0.6	--
1968	36,750	0.5	--	--
1970	44,674	0.5	--	--
1971	--	--	0.9	--
1972	53,585	0.6	1.1	--
1973	--	--	0.9	13,069
1974	59,394	0.6	0.9	13,374

Sources: U.S. Department of Health, Education and Welfare, Office for Civil Rights, "Racial and Ethnic Enrollment Data from Institutions of Higher Education," Fall, 1968, 1970, 1972, 1974 (Washington, D.C.: U.S. Government Printing Office, 1970, 1972, 1974, 1976); American Council on Education, "The American Freshman: National Norms," Fall, 1966, 1971, 1972, 1973, 1974 (Washington, D.C.: ACE, 1967, 1972, 1973, 1974, 1975); U.S. Department of the Interior, Bureau of Indian Affairs, Office of Indian Education Programs, Fiscal Year 1973 Statistics Concerning Indian Education and Fiscal Year 1974 Statistics Concerning Indian Education (Washington, D.C.: U.S. Government Printing Office, 1974, 1975).

However, as mentioned earlier, we feel that the Census Bureau estimate of the Native American population in this country is incorrect. Further, these data also may be complicated by the fact that many Hispanic American individuals are of Native American ancestry and may now be listing their major identity group as Native American instead of Hispanic American. Because of the relatively small size of the Native American population, a small shift in the ethnic identification of Hispanic Americans who are of Native American ancestry could possibly cause a dramatic shift in the number and percentage of college-age persons in the Native American category. A sizable number of Hispanic Americans do list their ancestry as Native American. If the American Freshmen National Norm data collected by the American Council on Education are correct, and we believe that they are, then they imply that there is a high Native American dropout rate early in their college life. For example, a survey of the entire college population by the Office for Civil Rights reported a 0.6 percent Native American enrollment, overall, for four years; while the American Council on Education reported a freshmen enrollment of 1.1 percent. Possible conclusions are that either there is a high dropout rate or the two sets of figures are not compatible. We believe that both sets of data are compatible and that there is a slightly higher than average college dropout rate among Native Americans.

In 1974, 22.5 percent (13,374) of all Native American undergraduate students were enrolled in BIA programs compared to 77.5 percent (59,394) who were enrolled in higher education programs not sponsored by the BIA.

In 1975, 3,906 or 0.3 percent of all graduate students in the United States were Native American. Within this total, 521 were enrolled in BIA programs. These data would suggest, based upon the 0.6 percent of Native Americans enrolled in undergraduate schools that Native Americans are underrepresented in graduate schools. In comparing the number of Native Americans enrolled in graduate schools in 1968 and 1974, we find 1,908 enrolled in 1968 compared to 3,906 in 1974, approximately a 62 percent increase.

Data from the BIA programs indicate that between 1973 and 1974 the undergraduate enrollment increased by 2.3 percent while support for graduate enrollment increased by 6.5 percent. This suggests that the BIA is either increasing its support for graduate studies (for students graduating from BIA programs) or that there is an increase in the number of Native American students graduating from college and qualifying for graduate studies. We believe it is due to the latter. For example, in 1973 only 770 students graduated from undergraduate school who were supported by the BIA, compared to 1,141 who graduated in 1974, a 48.2 percent increase. We believe the Native American undergraduate enrollment will remain rather stable over the next decade.

BLACKS

In 1974 the U.S. Bureau of the Census listed 24 million blacks
residing in the United States, constituting 11.4 percent of the total
U.S. population. In that same year the Census Bureau listed 814,000
blacks enrolled in colleges between the ages 14 and 34. This represented an increase of 8.4 percent from 1973 (see Table 3.6). While
these data are very enlightening, the story of higher education for
blacks started a long time ago.

The first black Americans came to the United States on a slave
ship a few years before the Pilgrims arrived at Plymouth in 1620.
Since that time blacks have been fighting against great odds to achieve
a full and meaningful existence in this country, with equality and free-
dom. Today, blacks are continuing their fight for a bigger share of
this country's resources through its colleges and universities. A
brief history of the black's involvement with institutions of higher
education in this country should highlight the problem.

In 1826, John Brown Russwurm of Bowdoin College in Maine
and Edward Jones of Amherst College in Massachusetts were the
first blacks to graduate from college in America (Pifer 1973). Harvard University, on the other hand, took 200 years before it graduated
blacks (Johnson 1969). From this small beginning blacks continued to
struggle for equality within institutions of higher education. Before
the Civil War only 28 blacks had graduated from college; 2,500
graduates by 1900; 31,090 graduates by 1936; 296,666 graduates in
the 1970s population (Johnson 1969). Even though there has been a
steady increase in absolute numbers, percentagewise blacks still
lag behind whites.

Periodically, efforts have been made to provide comprehensive
data on black college enrollment. The first major effort was made
by Charles S. Johnson in 1938 (Johnson 1969) to cover the years from
1914 to 1936; the second major effort was made by the U.S. Office of
Education (Brown 1942); and the next attempt was made by Fred
Crossland in 1971 (Crossland 1971) to cover the decade 1960 to 1970.
The Johnson study was originally published in 1938. Johnson's data
are very reliable as to racial identity, because during that period
every American received a racial identification tag.

The 1942 study by the U.S. Office of Education was also very
reliable, but it was confined primarily to a study of the black colleges in the South and Midwest along with a sampling of eight white
colleges in the North. The sampling of the eight white colleges was
conducted to ascertain how blacks were being treated and how many
blacks were enrolling in those colleges. However, these two studies
did not cover the total black college-age population.

TABLE 3.6

Black Undergraduate Enrollment, Summary Data

	1966	1967	1968	1969	1970	1971	1972	1973	1974
Total, U.S.[a] (Office for Civil Rights data)	--	--	535,134	--	585,021	--	772,560	--	921,218
Percent of college population	--	--	7.1	--	6.8	--	8.4	--	9.0
Total, U.S.[b] (U.S. Census data)	--	--	434,000	--	522,000	--	727,000	--	814,000
Percent of college population	--	--	6.4	--	7.0	--	8.7	--	9.2
Percent of freshmen who are black[c]	5.0	--	--	--	--	6.3	8.7	7.8	7.4
Enrollment in historically black colleges[d]	138,043	139,813	144,049	149,706	154,602	162,638	164,740	163,500	--

Sources: [a]U.S. Department of Health, Education and Welfare, Office for Civil Rights, "Racial and Ethnic Enrollment Data from Institutions of Higher Education," Fall, 1968, 1970, 1972, 1974 (Washington, D.C.: U.S. Government Printing Office, 1968, 1970, 1972, 1974).

[b]U.S. Bureau of the Census, Current Population Reports, "The Social and Economic Status of the Black Population in the United States, 1974," Series P-23, No. 54 (Washington, D.C.: U.S. Government Printing Office, 1975), Table 71.

[c]American Council on Education, "The American Freshman: National Norms," Fall, 1966, 1972, 1973, 1974 (Washington, D.C.: ACE, 1967, 1972, 1973, 1974, 1975).

[d]Elias Blake, Jr., et al., "Degrees Granted and Enrollment Trends in Historically Black Colleges: An Eight-Year Study" (Washington, D.C.: Institute for Services to Education, 1975).

The Crossland study, on the other hand, suffered from a failure of public agencies to identify individuals by race. One must re-
member that during the 1950s, 1960s, and the early 1970s racial
identification of individuals in this country was restricted or elim-
inated. Therefore, Crossland had to rely solely on a 5 percent
statistical sample of the population by the Census Bureau. Further,
the Census Bureau admitted to undercounting blacks by approximately 8 percent (Straus and Harkins 1974).

Our information on black college enrollment is different from
that of the other studies in that it makes use of the first national
survey of racial and ethnic enrollment in colleges and universities
(by the Department of Health, Education and Welfare, 1968 through
1974). The Department of Health, Education and Welfare (HEW) surveys made a complete head count of the college-age population. Also,
our study will document the college status of blacks for the most recent time period. It must be remembered that data from government
sources are published at least two years after the collection of the
data; therefore, a 1976 publication would include information on enrollment data no later than 1974.

The Census Bureau estimate of the 1974 black undergraduates
enrolled was a 55.9 percent increase over 1970. However glorious
these figures may seem, and the resulting percentage increase over
a four-year period by the Census Bureau, one must take a closer
look at other data sources. First, the Current Census Report is a
survey of approximately 2,500 households and it leaves it up to the
discretion of the interviewer to determine the race and ethnicity of
the individual being interviewed; second, there is a tendency on the
part of individual households to overestimate members of that family
who are enrolled in college. For example, it is not uncommon for
a mother to say that yes, my daughter is enrolled in college, when in
fact her daughter has been out of college for a semester or so. This
absence from college would have been detected by an actual head
count of the number of black students enrolled in college. Another
bit of information should be brought to light: There is a large number of Vietnam veterans returning to civilian life and taking advantage
of educational benefits under the GI Bill. Many are black veterans,
and this would seem to account for the swell in the black enrollment
between 1973 and 1974. For example, the Census Bureau indicated
that 8.4 percent of college enrollment was black in 1971, 8.7 percent in 1972, 8.4 percent in 1973, and 9.2 percent in 1974. This increase from 1971 to 1972 and then a decline in 1973 followed by a
huge increase in 1974 can only be explained by one of two factors:
there was an increase of local, state, and federal financial support
for minority college students or an increase in the number of veterans returning to college campuses or a combination of both. It is

our belief that this increase may be accounted for by a combination
of both.

While the Current Population Report by the Census Bureau indicates one figure for black undergraduate enrollment and other reports indicate different numbers and percentages, a national survey
by HEW's Office for Civil Rights indicated that in 1971 blacks constituted 6.8 percent of the student population compared to 8.4 percent
suggested by the Census; in 1973 HEW, in a survey of the complete
college-age population, also indicated an 8.4 percent which was
similar to that by the Census of 8.4 percent. However, in 1974 a
survey of the total population by HEW indicated an 8.6 percent enrollment, while the Census Bureau indicated 9.2 percent.

In addition to college enrollment figures published by the Census Bureau and HEW there are also figures published by the American Council on Education (ACE). ACE has since 1966 surveyed the
freshman class within U.S. colleges and universities. Their survey indicates that the percentage of black freshmen was 6.3 in 1971,
8.7 in 1972, 7.8 in 1973, and 7.4 in 1974. These data seem to be
at variance with data collected by the Census Bureau and show a
small difference with data collected by HEW. If one can believe the
ACE survey data then one must assume that most of the students
that constitute the rise above the ACE freshmen data are individuals
in the armed services who return to college as upperclassmen. This
would suggest that the ACE survey could not and did not account for
individuals who have been out of the system for several years but who
are now returning as upperclassmen rather than freshmen.

In terms of the true estimate of the number of black undergraduates we believe that the best estimate is that provided by HEW.
This survey made a head count of more than 95 percent of the college population, which is far superior to the survey of some 2,000
by the Census Bureau. ACE data only involved freshmen. If we accept this assumption, then the truest estimate of the black undergraduate population in the United States in 1974 was 772,560, which
constituted 8.4 percent of the undergraduate enrollment.

In keeping with our mode of analysis one would have to ask
this question: Is there significant black underrepresentation in institutions of higher education? The answer is definitely "yes," because if one looks at the data on the percentage of the black population between the ages of 14 and 24 years we find that the black percentage, 23.5, is 3 percent higher than that for the whites (see
Table 3.7). If we consider the variously reported number of blacks
in institutions not included in the survey we will find that the percentage is even higher. It has been estimated that approximately
15,000 black males are institutionalized, namely with the military
and in penal institutions. Whites are also in these institutions but

TABLE 3.7

The College-Age Population by Race

	1960	1970	1975*	1980*	1985*
All races					
14–24-year olds	27,347,000	40,593,000	44,520,000	45,195,000	42,222,000
Total population	180,671,000	204,879,000	213,450,000	222,769,000	234,068,000
Percent of total	15.1	19.8	20.9	20.3	18.0
Whites					
14–24-year olds	24,008,000	35,125,000	38,016,000	38,114,000	35,139,000
Total population	160,023,000	179,491,000	185,578,000	192,162,000	200,548,000
Percent of total	15.0	19.6	20.5	19.8	17.5
Blacks					
14–24-year olds	3,072,000	4,914,000	5,772,000	6,179,000	6,052,000
Total population	19,006,000	22,787,000	24,539,000	26,371,000	28,304,000
Percent of total	16.2	21.6	23.5	23.4	21.4

*Figures are projections.

Source: U.S. Bureau of the Census, Current Population Reports, "Characteristics of American Youth: 1974," Special Studies, Series P-23, No. 51 (Washington, D.C.: U.S. Government Printing Office, 1975).

their percentage representation is much smaller. Therefore, we
would have to conclude that the blacks are underrepresented in institutions of higher education. If we attempt to correlate equity for
blacks from the college-age availability pool, parity for blacks would
exceed their 11 percent representation of the total population. To
gain parity, the college representation among blacks should approxi-
mate 14 percent of the college-age population.

In terms of the availability pool for college we find that while
the high school graduation rate is lower for blacks than whites, the
percent distribution is not the entire story. In order to equate these
figures we would have to assume that the type and kind of schooling
available to all students, regardless of race, was randomly distributed
throughout the country. However, blacks are not randomly distributed
throughout the country; they are more urbanized than the general population (except for the Puerto Ricans and Asian Americans).

By and large, many black students attend fairly inadequate
schools in urban ghettos. We would just like to make the point that
it is not always the number of years of schooling completed that is
important but the kind and quality of that schooling. It would be difficult for a youngster to matriculate at the college level if he has not
been prepared for that level of instruction; and further it would be
more difficult for a black to gain entrance into an institution of higher
education if he has been programmed along a vocational track. On
the other hand, the many black students who were afforded an inferior elementary and secondary education but who are very bright
must be given a chance to attend college.

Beginning in the mid-1960s many academically talented but
educationally disadvantaged (low academic achievement) black students were allowed to enroll in colleges and universities with the
special assistance provided by "equal opportunity programs." These
equal opportunity programs were designed to assist educationally
disadvantages students with their social, academic, and financial
problems. Without these special programs, given the poor secondary
education received by many blacks, college success would have been
difficult; and without financial support provided by these programs
matriculation would not have been possible.

While there are a large number of blacks attending college in
the United States, the selectivity of institutions attended is lower
than that for the population in general. For example, at the university level only 3.9 percent of the student population is black; 8.7 percent is enrolled in four-year colleges; while 8.3 percent is enrolled
in two-year colleges. In short, blacks are overrepresented in four-
year and two-year colleges and underrepresented in universities
and graduate centers (see Table 3.8).

TABLE 3.8

Postsecondary School Enrollment of Persons 16 to 34 Years Old,
by Type of School, 1973

	All Races	Blacks	Whites
Persons 16 to 34 years old	61,546,000	7,152,000	53,464,000
Postsecondary students	8,524,000	678,000	7,659,000
Percent of total	14	9	14
Enrolled in college	7,354,000	549,000	6,639,000
University	4,032,000	252,000	3,698,000
Four-year college	1,570,000	134,000	1,386,000
Two-year college	1,752,000	163,000	1,555,000
Enrolled in vocational education school	1,170,000	128,000	1,020,000
Postsecondary students	8,524,000	678,000	7,659,000
Enrolled in college	86%	81%	87%
University	47	37	48
Four-year	18	20	18
Two-year	21	24	20
Enrolled in vocational education school	14	19	13
College students, excluding university	3,222,000	297,000	2,941,000
Enrolled in vocational education	47%	45%	47%
Public	25	36	23
Private	25	8	23
Enrolled in two-year college	53	55	53
Public	48	47	48
Private	3	5	3

Source: U.S. Bureau of the Census, Current Population Reports, "The Social and Economic Status of the Black Population in the United States, 1974," Special Studies, Series P-23, No. 54 (Washington, D.C.: U.S. Government Printing Office, 1975), Table 69.

Another problem that complicates black college enrollment figures is how does one estimate the number of black students enrolled in traditional college programs and degree credit programs. For example, 53 percent of black college students are enrolled in programs other than university and four-year colleges, compared to 38.8 percent for white students. It would be helpful to know what portion of that 53 percent of the black college population are enrolled in traditional two-year college transfer or degree credit programs, or what percent are enrolled in nontraditional college programs, such as credit-free courses or terminal vocational occupational programs. In many states where two-year colleges exist, the states usually reimburse local community colleges based upon student enrollment. Many of these institutions create novel and sometimes meaningless programs in order to attract disadvantaged students for enrollment purposes. These students in essence are admitted to human-interest type courses or one-shot-type educational adventures. Many of the students who attend these human-interest-created courses may be taking elementary school-level courses which carry the prestige of a college title.

If one considers college attendance as a process variable then it is important that we know what types of institutions blacks are being processed through (see Table 3.9). Process variables are important in the sense that students who graduate from high-status colleges and universities are more likely to be successful when seeking employment later on in life than those who are processed through lower-status institutions. What we are saying is that there is significant interaction between process variables and outcome variables. If we consider the process variable, type of college attended, and the output variable, we feel that graduation from a prestigious institution will do more to facilitate or advance one's career. Translated, black college graduates will still be at a substantial disadvantage in competing for choice career options if the black population is not equally distributed throughout the higher education hierarchy. The black college graduate even with his degree will still be at a disadvantage relative to the white college graduate unless he is allowed to matriculate and earn a represented number of degrees from higher-status institutions. We are not arguing for the status differential between institutions of higher education, we are merely stating that it exists; and because it exists black college students ought to be given equitable treatment in their distribution among the various institutions.

According to the Office for Civil Rights, in 1974 blacks represented about 9.0 percent of the total college enrollment or 921,218 college students (see Table 3.6). However, the black population in this country is 11 percent of the total population with a college-age population of 13 percent. Therefore, we conclude that the black is

TABLE 3.9

Weighted National Norms for Universities, Fall 1974

				Racial Background			
	White/ Caucasian	Black/Negro/ Afro-American	Native American	Asian American	Mexican American/ Chicano	Puerto Rican American	Other
Men							
Public universities							
Low selectivity	95.9	3.0	0.5	0.3	0.2	0.1	0.7
Medium selectivity	96.9	1.1	1.0	0.8	0.2	0.2	1.1
High selectivity	91.8	3.0	0.8	3.5	1.4	0.2	1.7
Private universities							
Low selectivity	93.9	3.3	0.2	1.1	0.3	0.8	2.1
Medium selectivity	90.6	3.8	0.9	1.3	2.7	0.6	2.0
High selectivity	92.6	3.7	0.6	2.4	0.9	0.5	1.9
Women							
Public universities							
Low selectivity	94.3	4.8	0.5	0.4	0.2	0.1	0.6
Medium selectivity	97.2	4.1	1.3	0.5	0.1	0.1	0.9
High selectivity	90.4	4.3	0.9	3.7	1.2	0.2	1.7
Private universities							
Low selectivity	92.1	5.3	0.7	0.9	0.3	0.9	1.9
Medium selectivity	90.4	5.3	0.5	1.3	1.8	0.4	1.8
High selectivity	90.0	7.0	0.8	1.7	0.5	0.3	1.6

Source: Alexander Astin et al., The American Freshman: National Norms for Fall 1974, Cooperative Institutional Research Program, American Council on Education (Los Angeles: University of California, Los Angeles, 1975).

severely underrepresented in institutions of higher education. If we
view parity in terms of the percentage of the population that are of
college age, we project that parity for the black community would
include 14 percent of the total college population with members of
the armed forces included. Further, while the black college enrollment has increased over the last five years we still find that the
black college students are underrepresented in the prestigious universities; and they are overrepresented in the lower-status institutions such as the small four-year colleges and the two-year colleges.

TABLE 3.10

College Enrollment, 3 to 34 Years Old,
October 1964 to October 1974
(numbers in thousands)

	All Races, Total	Whites		Blacks*	
		Total	Percent of Total	Total	Percent of Total
1964	4,644	4,338	93.4	306	6.6
1965	5,675	5,317	93.7	358	6.3
1966	6,085	5,708	93.8	377	6.2
1967	6,401	5,905	92.3	370	5.8
1968	6,801	6,255	92.0	434	6.4
1969	7,435	6,827	91.8	492	6.6
1970	7,413	6,759	91.2	522	7.0
1971	8,087	7,273	89.9	680	8.4
1972	8,313	7,458	89.7	727	8.7
1973	8,179	7,324	89.5	684	8.4
1974	8,827	7,781	88.1	814	9.2

*Data for 1964 to 1966 are for "blacks and other races."
Source: U.S. Bureau of the Census, Current Population Re-
ports, "School Enrollment--Social and Economic Characteristics of
Students: October, 1974," Series P-20, No. 278 (Washington, D.C.:
U.S. Government Printing Office, 1975).

We predict that the number and percentage of blacks enrolled
in colleges and universities will decline over the next four years.
This prediction is based upon a decline in the freshmen enrollment
for blacks from a high of 8.7 percent in 1972, to 7.8 percent in 1973,

and a low of 7.4 percent in 1974. We expect the enrollment over the next four years to taper off to about 8.4 percent of the college population from a high of 9.2 percent in 1974 as estimated by the Census Bureau and 9.0 percent as estimated by HEW.

There is one caution that all must take in viewing data on black enrollment for the decade between 1964 and 1974 (see Tables 3.6 and 3.10). If we look at the beginning of that decade we find that for the years 1964 to 1970 there was relatively little increase in the black college enrollment. In fact, from 1964 to 1968 there was a percentage decline. It was not until 1971 that we find a sharp rise in the black college enrollment. As previously mentioned, this rise probably resulted from black members of the armed forces returning home from the Vietnam conflict and taking advantage of educational benefits under the GI Bill. However, since 1971, the first year of the sharp rise in percentage of blacks attending college, the rate has remained rather constant. We make these suggestions so that the reader may share with us our concern about the cause of this rise at the beginning of the 1971 school year.

In 1974 about 35.4 percent of all black college students were enrolled in predominantly black colleges (20 percent in historically black colleges); and 64.6 percent of all black students were enrolled in integrated or nonblack colleges and universities (see Table 3.11).

TABLE 3.11

Total Enrollment, Fall 1974, and Degrees Conferred, 1971-72, in U.S. Institutions Attended Predominantly by Black Students

| | Number of Institutions | Total Enrollment | Earned Degrees Conferred | | |
			Bachelor's and First Professional	Master's	Doctorate
Four-year institutions					
All	90	197,284	26,270	4,951	28
Public	37	137,530	16,224	3,502	--
Private	53	59,754	10,046	1,449	28
Two-year institutions					
All	30	90,917	--	--	--
Public	20	88,678	--	--	--
Private	10	2,239	--	--	--
Total	120	288,201	26,270	4,951	28

Source: U.S. Department of Health, Education and Welfare, Digest of Educational Statistics, 1975 edition (Washington, D.C.: U.S. Government Printing Office, 1976), Table 90.

ASIAN AMERICANS

Asian Americans have been in the United States since the early 1800s. The original Asian immigrants came to this country mainly as a source of cheap labor on West Coast farms. Today approximately 1.0 percent of the total U.S. population is Asian American. Although the term Asian American is used, it is a broad term used to describe a variety of distinct ethnic groups: Japanese, Chinese, Filipino, and Hawaiian Americans. Further, there are other Asian groups not included in this study: Koreans, Vietnamese, and other people of Asian ancestry. In this book we will be concerned only with Japanese, Chinese, and Filipinos. The other Asian American groups are usually listed or combined with the total white population and thus will not be considered here. One shortcoming is that information generated by the U.S. Census on the Asian population is collected only every decade. Special studies by the Census Bureau such as those carried out among black and Spanish-speaking populations have not been conducted—at least they have never been produced up to the date of this report.

In 1970 the Census Bureau recorded that 588,324 Japanese, 431,538 Chinese, and 336,731 Filipino Americans lived in the United States. The history of the Asian people in the United States has been plagued with problems of immigration by exclusion in one form or another. In 1882 Congress passed the general immigration law excluding undesirable persons likely to become a public nuisance. And in 1882 Congress passed the Chinese Exclusion Act aimed specifically at prohibiting Chinese workers from entering the United States. One provision of the Chinese Exclusion Act stipulated that no state court shall admit Chinese to citizenship. Americans all but forgot the fact that it was during this time that the Chinese almost single-handedly built the western end of the Transcontinental Railroad, linking the eastern and western seaboards in 1885.

Congress passed another law in 1921 specifying that an alien-born woman marrying a U.S. citizen could no longer automatically assume citizenship via marriage. This prevented the largely male Asian population from returning to Japan and China to marry and bring their wives back to this country. The 1924 act, the Japanese Exclusion Act, tightened enforcement of these regulations in that alien-born married women were no longer allowed to enter to join their husbands. Although alien-born wives were not admissible as citizens, their children were. This produced long periods of separation between American male Asian citizens and their Chinese- or Japanese-born wives. Another part of the law stipulated that many American-born women who married men ineligible for citizenship lost their citizenship. Thus if a Chinese or Japanese female citizen

married a Japanese or Chinese male from abroad she would lose her
U.S. citizenship. This act was modified in 1932 by the Cable Act
which granted women so deprived of their citizenship the right to re-
gain it through naturalization.

In 1944 Congress repealed the Exclusion Act of 1882 but in doing so established an annual quota of 105 for persons of Asian ancestry. The Immigration Act of 1924 was amended in 1946 (the War
Brides Act) to allow alien wives of citizens admissible on a nonquota
basis. Alien wives and children of resident aliens were given preferential treatment beyond the quota limitations. In 1947 the War Brides
Act was amended to allow the entry of approximately 6,000 Chinese
women into the country. Finally, the Immigration Act of 1965
cleared the way for fair and equitable immigration to this country by
people of Asian descent (see Table 3.12).

TABLE 3.12

Immigrants Born in Specified Asian Countries and Areas, 1972

Country of Birth	1965	1972	Percent Change
China and Taiwan	4,057	17,339	+327.4
Japan	3,180	4,757	+49.6
Korea	2,165	18,876	+771.9
Philippines	3,130	29,376	+838.5
Western Samoa	--	199	--

Source: U.S. Department of Justice, Immigration and Naturalization Service, 1972 Annual Report.

Beginning in the 1920s, Filipinos came to the United States in
much the same pattern as the Chinese and Japanese, to be employed
as "stoop" farm laborers throughout the West Coast and Hawaii.
They worked in the agricultural fields, some as cannery workers in
California, Hawaii, and Alaska, while others served as domestics
in restaurants and hotels. The Filipinos, like the Chinese and
Japanese who migrated to this country before them, also experienced
an exclusion act, the 1934 Toidings-McDuffie Act, which severely
restricted further immigration into the United States by Filipinos.
And, like the Chinese and the Japanese, the first Filipinos who migrated to this country were mainly males who were forced to leave
their wives back in the Philippines.

Perhaps the cruelest of all the exclusion acts against Asian American people were those provisions which prevented the Asian males from bringing their wives with them to this country. This produced an unnatural setting in which families were separated and Asian males were left without female companionship. While a few Filipinos in California married Mexican American women, and a few Japanese and Chinese Americams married white women, a history of interethnic or interracial marriages remained very small. The problem of Asian males in this country without their wives is probably best highlighted by statistics from the Census Bureau for the Chinese Americans (see Table 3.13). In 1860 the ratio of Chinese males to females was 19 to 1; in 1880 it was 21 to 1; in 1900, 19 to 1; in 1930, 4 to 1; and as late as 1960, 1.3 to 1. Currently the Chinese male-female ratio is about even, 1.1 to 1.

TABLE 3.13

Sex Ratio of Chinese in the United States, 1860-1970

Year	Males per 100 Females	Male:Female Ratio (approximate)
1860	1,858	19:1
1870	1,284	13:1
1880	2,106	21:1
1900	1,887	19:1
1930	395	4:1
1940	285	3:1
1950	190	2:1
1960	133	1.3:1
1970	111	1.1:1

Source: U.S. Bureau of the Census, "Detail Characteristics: Census of Population, 1960" and "Japanese, Chinese, and Filipinos in the United States," Subject Reports, PC (2)-1G (Washington, D.C.: U.S. Government Printing Office, July 1973).

The 1965 Immigration Act made possible an increase in the Asians who immigrated to the United States. Between 1965 and 1972, Chinese immigration increased 327.4 percent, Japanese 49.6 percent, Korean 771.9 percent, and Filipino 838.5 percent. This immigration trend by people of Asian descent to the United States

probably will continue at a modest rate through the rest of the twentieth century, perhaps tapering off during the late 1980s or early
1990s. These immigration figures indicate a drastic change in the
makeup and demographics within the Asian American community.
We expect these immigration patterns to affect drastically educational need, enrollment, and educational attainment among Asian
Americans.

Data on Chinese Americans from the decennial Census from
1910 through 1970 illustrate this point (see Table 3.14). For almost
50 years the Chinese population experienced a modest increase,
then in 1970 it took a quantum leap, from 237,292 in 1960 to 431,583
in 1970. With the new immigration law in effect that figure is probably well over a half million in 1976.

TABLE 3.14

Chinese Population in the United States, 1910-70

Year	Population
1910	71,531
1920	61,639
1930	74,954
1940	77,504
1950	117,629
1960	237,292
1970	431,583

Source: U.S. Bureau of the Census, "Detail Characteristics:
Census of Population, 1960" and "Japanese, Chinese, and Filipinos
in the United States," Subject Reports, PC (2)-1G (Washington,
D.C.: U.S. Government Printing Office, July 1973).

While we have lumped the three Asian communities together,
they are not a monolithic group. This combining of Japanese,
Chinese, and Filipino Americans is due more to convenience than
to striking similarities between the groups. Data available on Asian
Americans from sources other than the Census Bureau are available
only in combined form, so the authors were forced in many ways to
combine the Asian American communities into one grouping. While
the Census Bureau data group Asian Americans into separate categories, its data is only available through the year 1970.

Median years of educational attainment for the three groups are 15.5 for Japanese Americans, 12.4 for Chinese Americans, and 12.2 for Filipino Americans. Median family incomes by ethnic groups are $12,515 for Japanese Americans, $10,610 for Chinese Americans, and $9,318 for Filipino Americans.

In 1974, 115,888 Asian Americans were enrolled in undergraduate institutions of higher education in the United States (see Table 3.15). This represented 1.1 percent of all undergraduate students in the United States, which compares to the Asian population representation of 0.8 percent. The 1974 freshman class consisted of 0.9 percent Asian Americans, representing a slight decline in entering freshman enrollment from the 1972 and 1973 school year. Figures on entering freshman enrollment from 1966 through 1974 reveal that beginning in 1972 we may have the first enrollment of Asians immigrated to this country since the passage of the 1965 Immigration Act. That is probably the best explanation for a 100 percent increase in Asian freshman enrollment between 1971 (0.5 percent) and 1972 (1.1 percent).

TABLE 3.15

Asian American Undergraduate Enrollment, Summary Data

	Total, U.S.[a]	Percent of College Population	Percent of Freshmen Who Are Asian American[b]
1966	--	---	0.7
1968	55,095	0.7	--
1970	87,971	1.0	--
1971	--	--	0.5
1972	95,714	1.0	1.1
1973	--	--	0.9
1974	115,888	1.1	0.9

Sources: [a]U.S. Department of Health, Education and Welfare, Office for Civil Rights, "Racial and Ethnic Enrollment Data from Institutions of Higher Education," Fall, 1968, 1970, 1972, 1974 (Washington, D.C.: U.S. Government Printing Office, 1968, 1970, 1972, 1974).

[b]American Council on Education, "The American Freshman: National Norms," Fall, 1966, 1972, 1973, 1974 (Washington, D.C.: ACE, 1967, 1972, 1973, 1974, 1975).

At first glance, a look at the Asian American representation in college and in the general population may cause one to conclude that Asian Americans are overrepresented in institutions of higher education. However, that assumption is far from being correct. Asian Americans have a higher high school graduate rate than any other group in the United States. While the high school graduation rate for the total United States is 52.3, rates for the different Asian American groups are 68.8 for Japanese, 57.8 for Chinese, and 54.7 for Filipinos. These data suggest to us that the Asian Americans are not overrepresented in institutions of higher education but indeed may be underrepresented given their high school graduation rates. Since we are talking about enrollment in institutions of higher education, the high secondary school graduate rate does not tell the whole story.

It is not just the percentage of Asian Americans who graduate from high school, it is the fact that among all high school graduates Asian American high school graduates have generally graduated in the academic top half of their class. It is this factor that leads us to conclude that an even higher percentage of Asians should be enrolled in our colleges and universities.

We can speculate as to why the Asian American community has such a high graduation rate and, further, why those who graduate are among the top academic achievers. One speculation is (and we believe this to be valid) that the uneven distribution of males to females within the Asian community gave the community added resources. It is our belief that these added resources resulted in the freeing of human resources which stimulated young people within the Asian American communities to attend school and to do well in their studies. However, now that these resources no longer are available to the Asian American communities (the unequal distribution of males to females) we believe that past patterns of high secondary school graduation rates and academic achievement will, in the future, look more like that for the American population in general. Another speculation is that Asian Americans in general are urban dwellers and as such their academic achievement reflects the higher-than-average achievement for urban dwellers. In short, Asian American communities in the United States do not represent a random distribution of the population throughout the United States. They are located mainly in the more advanced states in terms of educational systems--California, New York, Washington, and Hawaii. They are also located mainly in urban areas with excellent school systems (at least they were outstanding prior to the 1970 census), namely, San Francisco, Bakersfield, Los Angeles, Honolulu, Seattle, and Portland.

We believe that while at present the Asian American community is adequately represented in institutions of higher education, the future may hold a few problems. Internally, the older Asian American communities may continue to expect the same academic productivity among Asian American students that characterized their achievement prior to the passage of the 1965 Immigration Act. Externally, the general public may expect the same academic productivity from Asian American students as in the past.

However, problems that new immigrants bring to this country are more likely to be similar to those experienced by Hispanic Americans. These immigrants are likely to experience bilingual and bicultural educational problems. In addition they may experience culture shock. We stress these concerns because we feel strongly that educational institutions will and ought to plan ahead to face the problems that are likely to emanate from this drastic change of character within Asian American communities.

HISPANIC AMERICANS

In 1975 approximately 5.3 percent of the U.S. population (11,202,000) represented individuals of Spanish origin (see Table 3.16). The Hispanic American population is not a single group but is composed of several ethnic groups: 3.2 percent Mexican Americans, 0.8 percent Puerto Ricans, 0.4 percent Cubans, 0.3 percent Central Americans, and 0.7 percent other Spanish-origin individuals. Most Hispanic Americans have one thing in common: most of them came from Spanish-speaking countries and use Spanish as their first language. However, many Hispanic Americans are just as fluent in the English language.

The largest Hispanic American group is Mexican Americans who reside mainly in the five southwestern states of the United States: Arizona, California, Colorado, New Mexico, and Texas. The Census Bureau often refers to Hispanic Americans in these states as "Spanish surnamed." Hispanic Americans outside of the five southwestern states carry the common designation "Spanish origin." Approximately 16.7 percent of all individuals in the five southwestern states are Spanish-surnamed individuals (see Table 3.17).

Most Spanish-surnamed are Mexican Americans who immigrated to this country or gained their citizenship by the Treaty of Guadalupe Hidalgo in 1848. That treaty, signed between the United States and the government of Mexico, granted U.S. citizenship to all residents who lived in the territory conceded to the United States by the Mexican government following the Mexican American War.

TABLE 3.16

Hispanic American Population in the United States
by Type of Spanish Origin, March 1975

Origin	Total	Percent Distribution		College Age, 18-24 Years	Median Age in Years
		Total Population	Hispanic American Population		
Hispanic Americans	11,202,000	5.3	100.0	13.2	20.7
Mexican	6,690,000	3.2	59.7	14.4	19.8
Puerto Rican	1,671,000	0.8	14.9	12.0	19.4
Cuban	743,000	0.4	6.6	9.4	37.3
Central or South American	671,000	0.3	6.0	12.0	24.6
Other Spanish	1,428,000	0.7	12.7	11.1	20.2
All persons	209,572,000	100.0	--	12.6	28.6

Source: U.S. Bureau of the Census, Current Population Reports, "Persons of Spanish Origin in the United States: March 1975," Series P-20, No. 283 (Washington, D.C.: U.S. Government Printing Office, 1975), Tables 1 and 2.

Residing in the states of Arizona, California, Colorado, Texas, and New Mexico were many Mexican people, many of whom had lived in those states for centuries. Upon signing of the treaty many elected to remain on their land and become U.S. citizens.

TABLE 3.17

Hispanic Americans in the United States and
Selected Areas in March 1974

Area	Hispanic Americans[a]	Percent Hispanic American Population	
		1974 Current Population Survey[a]	1970 Census[b]
United States	10,795,000	5.2	4.5
Selected areas			
New York State	1,485,000	8.3	7.4
Five Southwestern states	6,319,000	16.7	13.9
California	3,153,000	15.4	11.9
Texas	2,099,000	17.8	16.4
Other[c]	1,067,000	18.9	16.0
Rest of the United States	2,991,000	1.9	1.8

[a]Resident population excludes persons in institutions and armed forces in barracks.
[b]Resident population.
[c]Arizona, Colorado, and New Mexico.
Source: U.S. Bureau of the Census, Current Population Reports, "Persons of Spanish Origin in the United States: March 1975," Series P-20, No. 280 (Washington, D.C.: U.S. Government Printing Office, April 1975), Table A.

Many Mexican Americans first came to this country to participate in a farm work program. This (Bracero) program was established by an agreement between the Mexican and the U.S. governments to provide cheap labor needed by American farmers. Although Mexican Americans came to the southwestern part of the United States to work as farm laborers, today most of them live in urban centers.

The next largest group of Hispanic Americans is Puerto Rican Americans (see Table 3.18). Unlike the other Hispanic American groups, Puerto Ricans have always (since 1917) been U.S. citizens because Puerto Rico enjoys Commonwealth status within the U.S. government. They have not had to deal with such immigration problems as the exclusionary acts passed by Congress against the Chinese and the Japanese.

Most Puerto Ricans who live on the mainland first migrated to New York City and then spread into surrounding states such as New Jersey, Connecticut, and Pennsylvania. A majority of Puerto Ricans on the mainland are still located in New York City (see Table 3.19); however, the trend does show a slight movement to other areas. There are now sizable Puerto Rican communities as far away as Chicago and California.

The next largest group of Hispanic Americans in the United States is Cubans, most of whom came to this country after the Cuban Revolution of the late 1950s. Cubans are much older than the average Hispanic Americans, their median age being 31.7 compared to 24.2 for Mexican Americans and 22.1 for Puerto Rican Americans. The Cuban American population also has a higher-than-average median educational attainment--10.3 years of school compared to 8.1 for Mexican Americans, 8.6 for Puerto Rican Americans, and 9.1 overall for all Hispanic Americans. Cubans who immigrated to the United States were drawn largely from middle- and upper-class families, ones with a higher-than-average level of education.

Hispanic Americans are composed of many races and ethnic backgrounds (see Table 3.20). Of them, 93.3 percent list their race as white, 5 percent black, and 0.3 percent Native American. Among Mexican Americans, 98.1 percent are white, 0.5 percent are black, and 0.4 percent are Native American. Among Puerto Ricans 92.6 percent are white, 5.3 are black, and 0.1 percent are Native American. Among the Cuban Americans 96 percent are white, 3.1 percent are black, and 0.9 percent are composed of other racial groups. Among the people of "Spanish surname," which includes mainly Mexican Americans living in the five southwestern states, 96.6 percent are white, 0.9 percent are Native Americans, and 2.4 percent belong to other racial groups. Data on the Spanish surnamed individuals are very interesting because many Spanish surnamed individuals listed their race as Native American, Filipino, and others. This designation of Spanish surname may explain some undercounting of the Native American population since many Native Americans in the southwest have Spanish surnames.

TABLE 3.18

Hispanic American Population by Sex and Type of Spanish Origin, for the
United States and Five Southwestern States, March 1974

Area and Origin	Total		Male		Female	
	Number	Percent	Number	Percent	Number	Percent
United States, total	10,795,000	100.0	5,285,000	100.0	5,510,000	100.0
Mexican	6,455,000	59.8	3,259,000	61.7	3,196,000	58.0
Puerto Rican	1,548,000	14.3	717,000	13.6	830,000	15.1
Cuban	689,000	6.4	326,000	6.2	362,000	6.6
Central or South American	705,000	6.5	341,000	6.5	364,000	6.6
Other Spanish	1,398,000	13.0	641,000	12.1	757,000	13.7
Five southwestern states	6,319,000	100.0	3,128,000	100.0	3,191,000	100.0
Mexican	5,453,000	86.3	2,730,000	87.3	2,723,000	85.3
Puerto Rican	62,000	1.0	28,000	0.9	33,000	1.0
Other Spanish*	806,000	12.8	370,000	11.8	436,000	13.7

*Includes Cuban, Central or South American, and other Spanish origin.

Source: U.S. Bureau of the Census, Current Population Reports, "Persons of Spanish Origin in the United States: March 1974," Series P-20, No. 280 (Washington, D.C.: U.S. Government Printing Office, 1975), Table 1.

TABLE 3.19

Persons of Puerto Rican Birth or Parentage in the United States and
in New York City, 1950-70

	United States			New York City		
	Total	Increase	Percent Change	Total	Increase	Percent Change
Puerto Rican birth or parentage						
1970	1,391,463	498,950	55.9	817,712	205,138	33.5
1960	892,513	591,138	196.1	612,574	366,694	149.1
1950	301,375	--	--	245,880	--	--
Puerto Rican birth						
1970	810,087	193,030	31.3	473,300	43,590	10.1
1960	617,056	390,946	172.9	429,710	242,290	129.3
1950	226,110	--	--	187,420	--	--
Puerto Rican parentage						
1970	581,376	305,919	111.1	344,412	161,548	88.3
1960	275,457	200,192	266.0	182,864	124,404	212.8
1950	75,265	--	--	58,460	--	--

Source: U.S. Bureau of the Census, Subject Reports, Puerto Ricans in the United States, PC (2) – IE, June 1973, Table 1.

TABLE 3.20

Hispanic Americans by Race, for the United States, 1970

Race	All Hispanic Americans	Persons of Mexican Origin	Persons of Puerto Rican Origin	Persons of Cuban Origin	Persons of Spanish Surname[a]
Number					
White	8,466,126	4,446,584	1,323,537	522,623	4,511,031
Black	454,934	24,148	75,920	17,151	--
Native American	26,859	15,988	1,038	161	43,517
Filipino	2,381	1,156	130	355	43,319
Other[b]	122,302	44,559	28,771	4,310	70,108
Total	9,072,602	4,532,435	1,429,396	544,600	4,667,975
Percent of total					
White	93.3	98.1	92.6	96.0	96.6
Black	5.0	0.5	5.3	3.1	--
Native American	0.3	0.4	0.1	--	0.9
Filipino	--	--	--	0.1	0.9
Other[b]	1.3	1.0	2.0	0.8	1.5

[a]Spanish surname individuals in five Southwestern states, Arizona, California, Colorado, New Mexico, and Texas.

[b]"Other" includes Blacks, Asians, and Hawaiians.

Source: U.S. Bureau of the Census, Subject Reports, Persons of Spanish Origin, PC (2) – 1C and PC (2) – 1D, June 1973, Table 1.

The race of Hispanic Americans continues to be confusing to analysts and researchers. For example, a field study by trained interviewers resulted in the following classifications: 608 white, 307 mulatto, and 80 black (Cordasco and Bucchioni 1972); while the respondents themselves classified 537 white, 397 mulatto, and 55 black. If we take a look at how the expert interviewers classified the 1,000 heads of households we find that 61 percent were white, 39 percent nonwhite. On the other hand, if we take a look at how the 1,000 respondents classified themselves, we find that 54 percent classified themselves as white, while 46 percent classified themselves as nonwhite. However, if we combine white and mulatto we find that the trained interviewers classified the population as 92 percent white or mulatto and 8 percent black. If we look at how the respondents classify themselves with respect to this combined category we find that 94.4 percent classified themselves as either white or mulatto compared to 5.6 percent who classified themselves as being black. The latter classification conforms quite well with the racial classification given by Puerto Rican individuals to U.S. Census takers: 95 percent white and 5 percent black.

Racial classification is important to the degree that while the individual may consider himself white, the general population does not recognize mulatto as a racial classification. Therefore, Puerto Ricans who are not considered white by the general population may be victims of racism similar to that exhibited against black and other nonwhite Americans.

In 1974, 287,032 Hispanic Americans were enrolled in college, which represented 2.8 percent of the college enrollment population (see Table 3.21). A six-year trend analysis, 1968-74, of Hispanic American undergraduate enrollment indicates an increase from 1.7 percent in 1968 to 2.8 percent in 1974. However, data on entering college freshman enrollment also indicates an increase in Hispanic American enrollment: in 1971 the Mexican American freshman enrollment was 1.1 percent compared to 1.5 percent in 1972, 1.3 percent in 1973, and 1.5 percent in 1974. This was also true for Puerto Rican Americans: in 1971, 0.2 percent of all freshmen were Puerto Ricans compared to 0.6 percent in 1972, 0.4 percent in 1973, and 0.6 percent in 1974. However, we feel that the percentage of Hispanic American undergraduate enrollment will stabilize at about 1.5 percent of the total college population for Mexican Americans and 0.6 percent for Puerto Rican Americans. There is nothing that gives evidence that these percentages are likely to increase in the near future for these two groups.

It seems clear to us that Hispanic Americans are severely underrepresented in institutions of higher education in the United States. A partial explanation for this may be explained by the rather

TABLE 3.21

Hispanic American Undergraduate Enrollment, Summary Data

	1968	1970	1971	1972	1973	1974
Total[a]	107,958	174,174	--	217,505	--	287,032
Percent of college population[a]	1.7	2.1	--	2.4	--	2.8
Percent of freshmen, Mexican American[b]						
All undergraduates	--	--	1.1	1.5	1.3	1.5
Two-year colleges	--	--	--	--	--	2.8
Four-year colleges	--	--	--	--	--	0.7
Universities	--	--	--	--	--	0.5
Percent of freshmen, Puerto Rican American[b]						
All undergraduates	--	--	0.2	0.6	0.4	0.6
Two-year colleges	--	--	--	--	--	0.8
Four-year colleges	--	--	--	--	--	0.8
Universities	--	--	--	--	--	0.2

Note: In March 1975, Hispanic Americans comprised 5.3 percent of the total U.S. population; broken down, Mexican Americans comprised 3.2 percent, Puerto Rican Americans, 0.8 percent.

Sources: [a]U.S. Department of Health, Education and Welfare, Office for Civil Rights, "Racial and Ethnic Enrollment Data from Institutions of Higher Education," Fall, 1968, 1970, 1972, 1974 (Washington, D.C.: U.S. Government Printing Office, 1968, 1970, 1972, 1974).

[b]American Council on Education, "The American Freshman: National Norms," Fall, 1966, 1972, 1973, 1974 (Washington, D.C.: ACE, 1967, 1972, 1973, 1974, 1975).

low percentage of Hispanic Americans who graduate from high
school: 22.1 percent for Puerto Ricans, 24.2 percent for Mexican
Americans, compared to 52.3 percent for the total United States
(see Table 3.22). The Hispanic Americans of Cuban ancestry may be
considered an exception to these data because, as stated earlier,
most Cuban Americans are much older and have higher educational
attainment. The Cuban population has a high school graduation rate
of 43.9 percent--almost double that for the other Hispanic American
groups.

TABLE 3.22

Years of School Completed by Hispanic Americans 14 Years Old
and Over, United States, March 1974

| | Schooling Completed | | | |
| | High School | College | | |
Origin	Four Years	One to Three Years	Four Years or More	Total
Mexican origin	804,000	243,000	95,000	3,989,000
Percent	20.2	6.1	2.4	100.0
Puerto Rican origin	178,000	28,000	31,000	951,000
Percent	18.7	6.2	3.3	100.0
Other Spanish origin, including Cuban, Central and South American, and other	307,000	251,000	150,000	1,916,000
Percent	28.3	13.1	7.8	100.0
Total Hispanic American	2,273,000	555,000	275,000	6,857,000
Percent	33.2	8.1	4.0	100.0

Source: U.S. Bureau of the Census, Current Population Reports, "Persons of Spanish Origin in the United States: March
1974," Series P-20, No. 280 (Washington, D.C.: U.S. Government Printing Office, 1975), pp. 38-39.

The low high school graduation rate among Hispanic Americans may be explained by poverty and racism. The whole issue of bilingual and bicultural education, if dealt with adequately, could do much to increase the number of Hispanic American high school graduates. In addition, many Hispanic American children bring to the school system another concern, namely, one of having a first language other than English. We feel strongly that the bilingual and bicultural needs of these children must be dealt with more aggressively and extensively at the preschool, elementary, and secondary levels. Guidance and counseling by other language-dominant professionals must be given. If these needs are not attended to, we feel that Hispanic Americans will continue to exhibit a rather low high school graduation rate.

We also support the notion that colleges and universities also should assist Hispanic American freshmen and sophomores in dealing with the bicultural nature of their life experiences. Teacher training should utilize research dealing with unique learning styles and strengths of the bilingual child. We find that colleges and universities have excluded themselves from this area of concern. They have concluded, incorrectly, that the problem of bilingualism and biculturalism is the almost exclusive domain of elementary and secondary schools.

While the percentage of Hispanic American students has increased (see Tables 3.23 and 3.24) over the last several years, they are disproportionately represented in the less-prestigious two- and four-year colleges. We find that only 23.4 percent of these students are enrolled in universities, compared to 34.7 percent for the United States as a whole; in four-year colleges, 55 percent compared to 76.8 percent, and in two-year colleges, 45 percent compared to only 23.2 percent. However, this rather high enrollment in two-year colleges may be explained somewhat by the large percentage of Hispanic Americans who live in California and other Southwestern states with large and extensive community college systems. However, Hispanic American two-year college enrollment far exceeds the percentage of white students from the Southwestern states enrolled in those institutions.

The enrollment by Hispanic American students in the less prestigious institutions will have implications later on in their lives in that it will affect their ability to compete with the general population for status positions. It will also have implications for advanced graduate studies, getting into graduate and professional schools.

We conclude that over the next decade the Hispanic American college enrollment will remain steady at about 1.5 percent. There is little evidence to indicate that there will be an increase in this percentage over the next several years, in fact we expect a slight

TABLE 3.23

Undergraduate College Enrollment of Persons 14 to 34 Years Old by Type of College, Year, Spanish Origin, and Age, October 1972
(civilian noninstitutional population)

Age, Race, and Spanish Origin	Type of College			Not Reported	Total Undergraduates[b]
	Two-Year[a]	Four-Year			
		First and Second Year	Third and Fourth Year		
14 to 34 years old					
Total	1,910,000	2,349,000	2,506,000	227,000	6,992,000
White	1,670,000	2,088,000	2,308,000	180,000	6,245,000
Black[c]	200,000	229,000	168,000	43,000	640,000
Spanish origin[d]	102,000	53,000	56,000	11,000	223,000
Percent					
Total	27.3	33.6	35.8	3.2	100.0
White	26.7	33.4	37.0	2.9	100.0
Black[c]	31.3	35.8	26.3	6.7	100.0
Spanish origin[d]	45.7	23.8	25.1	4.9	100.0
35 years old and over					
Total	216,000	83,000	131,000	4,000	434,000
Percent	49.8	19.1	30.2	0.9	100.0

[a]Includes 154,000 persons in two-year colleges enrolled in the third year of college.

[b]From 1966 to 1972 the college enrollment increased 22.6 percent: 2 percent for four-year colleges, and 67.8 percent for two-year colleges. Overall, two-year colleges accounted for 93.8 percent of the enrollment increase.

[c]The proportion of black undergraduates attending two-year colleges in 1972 was also somewhat higher than for whites.

[d]Hispanic Americans may be of any race. In October 1972, 46 percent of Hispanic American undergraduates were enrolled in two-year colleges, compared with 27 percent of all undergraduates. This high rate of two-year college attendance for Hispanic Americans may be explained partially because of the large proportion of Hispanic Americans who live in the West, where two-year college enrollment is more likely for all persons.

Source: U.S. Bureau of the Census, Current Population Reports, "Social and Economic Characteristics of Students: October 1973," Series P-20, No. 272 (Washington, D.C.: U.S. Government Printing Office, 1974), p. 2.

TABLE 3.24

Percent Undergraduate Enrollment, Total United States and Five Selected States, 1968-74

States	Native American	Black	Asian American	Hispanic American	White
California					
1968	0.5	5.6	3.8	5.5	84.6
1970	1.0	5.6	4.8	6.2	82.4
1972	0.9	6.5	4.7	6.9	80.8
1974	1.0	7.8	4.1	8.3	78.9
Florida					
1968	0.6	7.4	0.3	4.6	87.2
1970	0.2	8.8	0.4	3.2	87.4
1972	0.1	9.8	0.3	2.6	86.9
1974	0.2	9.4	0.3	2.4	87.6
Illinois					
1968	0.4	5.3	0.8	0.7	92.9
1970	0.5	6.8	0.8	0.8	91.1
1972	0.3	11.2	0.7	1.1	86.4
1974	0.2	14.1	0.8	1.6	83.2
New York					
1968	0.2	3.2	0.8	1.3	94.5
1970	0.3	5.4	1.0	2.0	91.3
1972	0.2	8.5	1.1	3.4	86.5
1974	0.3	10.7	1.3	4.3	83.6
Texas					
1968	1.1	7.5	0.6	7.5	83.2
1970	0.6	7.9	0.5	7.9	83.0
1972	0.6	9.0	0.5	9.1	80.6
1974	0.5	9.0	0.5	11.4	78.6
U.S. Total					
1968	0.6	5.8	1.0	1.9	90.7
1970	0.5	6.5	1.1	2.0	89.8
1972	0.6	8.4	1.0	2.4	87.6
1974	0.6	9.0	1.1	2.8	86.5

Source: U.S. Department of Health, Education and Welfare, Office for Civil Rights, "Racial and Ethnic Enrollment Data from Institutions of Higher Education," 1968, 1970, 1972, and 1974.

decline. It can be expected that the number of Hispanic American males taking advantage of GI benefits will decline during the next two years and will be exhausted in the next four years, thus returning the Hispanic American enrollment to normal. In sum, we find that these groups are severely underrepresented in U.S. colleges and universities at every level.

4

BACHELOR'S DEGREES EARNED

In a society that places such great value on academic credentials, the "bottom line" is an earned degree. Minorities have not
fared well, in terms of the number and percentage who have earned
bachelor's degrees from institutions of higher education in the
United States. In 1974, Native Americans represented 0.6 percent
of the college enrollment but received only 0.3 percent of bachelor's
degrees awarded; blacks constituted 8.4 percent of the college enrollment, but received only 5.2 percent of all bachelor's degrees
awarded; Asian Americans constituted 1.0 percent of the college
population and received 1.0 percent of all bachelor's degrees awarded;
while Hispanic Americans comprised 2.4 percent of the college enrollment but received only 1.2 percent of all bachelor's degrees
awarded (see Table 4.1).

The percentage of earned bachelor's degrees was computed by
considering only the percentage of minorities who had completed
four years in college. The white population received 87.7 percent
of all bachelor's degrees earned for 92.1 percent of total enrollment.

The disparity between the percentage of minorities enrolled in
college and those who remain long enough to earn degrees may be
because a disproportionate percentage of Native Americans, blacks,
and Hispanic Americans have enrolled in two-year colleges. Also,
many of these students have less-than-adequate preparation for college work. Many students listed as being college enrolled persons,
at the two-year college level, are enrolled in nondegree credit programs (see Table 4.2). Therefore, we feel that they should not be
included in the college enrollment data, maybe in a separate category called general postsecondary. Further, the community college
dropout rate is higher than that for four-year colleges and universities (Astin 1975). On the other hand, evidence suggests that the

staying power of minorities who reach upper divisional status is
similar to that for whites (Bayer 1972). Minority students who
reach their junior or senior year in college are just as likely to
graduate from college as white college students (see Table 4.3).

TABLE 4.1

Estimates of Bachelor's Degrees Earned, 1968-74,
from U.S. Institutions of Higher Education

	1968	1970	1972	1974
Native Americans (0.49%)	3,547	4,090	4,492	4,598
Blacks (5.2%)	37,810	43,603	47,882	49,017
Asian Americans (0.10%)	7,478	8,623	9,469	9,694
Hispanic Americans (1.2%)	8,814	10,164	11,162	11,426
Whites (92.1%)	670,518	773,249	849,125	869,264
Total	728,160	839,730	922,130	944,000

Notes: Subtotals may not equal totals due to rounding.
        Estimates were based on the percentage of minority
students in their fourth year of college as computed by the Office
for Civil Rights in 1970. While there have been small variations
in the percentage of minority students enrolled overall, the authors
feel that the percentage of minority students reaching upper division
status has remained relatively constant.

Sources: U.S. Office of Education, National Center for
Education Statistics, Educational Statistics; and Department of
Health, Education and Welfare, "Institutions of Higher Education,
1970," Report BI Final, unpublished.

TABLE 4.2

Associate Degrees, Diplomas, and Other Awards Based on Less Than Four Years
of Work Beyond High School, 50 States and District of Columbia, 1970

Race and Enrollment Percent	Associate Degrees Total	Two-Year Occupational Awards	Less Than Two-Year Awards	Total Terminal Occupational Competence Awards
Native Americans (0.7)	1,541	806	202	1,008
Blacks (8.3)	17,110	8,945	2,240	11,188
Asian Americans (1.4)	2,958	1,547	387	1,934
Spanish surnamed (4.2)	8,302	4,337	1,087	5,422
Total minority (14.5)	29,894	15,637	3,913	19,548
Whites (85.5)	176,129	92,118	23,056	115,174
Total	206,023	107,753	26,969	134,722

Sources: U.S. Department of Health, Education and Welfare, Office of Education, Associate Degrees and Other Formal Awards Below the Baccalaureate, 1969-70, 1972; and U.S. Department of Health, Education and Welfare, Office for Civil Rights, "Racial and Ethnic Enrollment Data from Institutions of Higher Education, Fall 1970," Table II-43A, 1972. Estimates are based upon enrollment in two-year colleges only.

TABLE 4.3

Resident Undergraduate Enrollment for Ethnic Groups by Year Enrolled, Full Time and Part Time, 50 States and District of Columbia, 1970

Year of Schooling and Level	Native Americans (.4)*	Blacks (11.1)	Asian Americans (.8)	Hispanic Americans (4.6)	Total Minority (16.8)	Whites (83.2)
First year	12,519	171,969	21,022	53,714	259,224	1,819,152
Percent	45.3	48.2	38.5	51.2	47.6	39.2
Second year	6,803	91,837	14,687	27,846	141,173	1,213,578
Percent	24.6	25.7	26.9	26.6	26.0	26.1
Third year	4,161	48,493	10,046	12,298	75,628	820,937
Percent	15.0	13.6	18.4	12.3	13.9	17.7
Fourth year	4,178	44,537	8,808	10,382	67,905	789,810
Percent	15.1	12.5	16.1	9.9	12.5	17.0
Lower division	19,322	263,806	35,709	81,560	400,397	3,032,730
Percent	69.9	73.9	65.4	77.8	73.6	65.3
Upper division	8,339	93,030	18,854	23,310	143,533	1,610,747
Percent	30.1	26.1	35.6	22.2	26.4	34.7
Total	27,661	356,836	54,563	104,870	543,930	4,643,477

*Figures in parentheses show percent of population.

Source: U.S. Department of Health, Education and Welfare, "Institutions of Higher Education, 1970, Constituent Institutions," 1970, Report BI Final, Table II-36A, unpublished.

BLACKS

Black college graduates in the United States are unique in that
many earned their degrees from historically black colleges (see
Table 4.4). In 1972, 47,882 black Americans earned bachelor's
degrees. About 52.2 percent were earned from historically black
colleges; 47.8 percent from white colleges and universities (see
Table 4.5). The fact that only 35 percent of all black college students are enrolled in black colleges, yet 52.2 percent of all degrees
earned by blacks are awarded by historically black colleges, may be
explained by the fact that many blacks enrolled in non-black colleges
are in two-year colleges. If one were to pursue this line of thought
further it is possible to conclude that a majority of all upper divisional
black college students are to be found in the historically black colleges. Therefore, it seems a fair conclusion that while most black
students are enrolled in white colleges, the historically black colleges will continue to have unequal influence in the preparation of
the black professionals. In short, the black colleges are still the
"backbone" of the black academic community. Many predominantly
black colleges now found in many northern states (many of which
are predominantly black two-year colleges) are not included among
the historically black colleges.

During the 1960s there were repeated demands by minorities
for college ethnic studies programs, and in the late 1960s and early
1970s many such programs were instituted in colleges and universities around the country. We are just now beginning to get data
regarding the output of those programs in terms of earned degrees
conferred (see Table 4.6). In 1974, 414 degrees were conferred in
the area of Afro-American or black studies: 392 were bachelor's
degrees, 19 master's degrees, and 3 doctoral degrees; 20 bachelor's
degrees were conferred in American Indian studies; 123 degrees in
Mexican American cultural studies were conferred: 111 bachelor's
degrees and 12 master's degrees; and 2,090 degrees in urban studies
were conferred: 1,289 were bachelor's degrees, 794 master's degrees, and 7 doctoral degrees. The rather small number of degrees
conferred in ethnic studies would suggest that while many minority
students are enrolled in ethnic study courses, they are receiving
their degrees in the traditional disciplines. The exception would be
urban studies, which may or may not be considered under the rubric
of ethnic studies.

TABLE 4.4

Number of Baccalaureate Degrees Awarded in Historically Black Colleges
by Selected Fields, 1965-66 to 1972-73

	1965-66	1966-67	1967-68	1968-69	1969-70	1970-71	1971-72	1972-73
Biological sciences	1,050	933	1,049	1,138	1,109	1,169	1,060	872
Business and management	772	930	1,251	1,793	2,490	3,215	3,490	3,793
Education	7,065	6,773	6,914	7,558	8,197	8,430	8,630	8,369
Physical sciences	402	383	373	391	447	338	433	415
Social sciences	2,705	2,889	3,332	4,167	5,049	5,453	5,476	4,915
Other	3,734	3,741	4,266	5,031	5,394	5,304	5,914	6,730
Total	15,728	15,649	17,185	20,078	22,686	24,039	24,976	25,094

Source: Elias Blake, Jr. et al., Degrees Granted and Enrollment Trends in Historically Black Colleges: An Eight-Year Study, Vol. 1, no. 1 (Washington, D.C.: Institute for Services to Education, Inc., October 1974), p. 37.

TABLE 4.5

Percentage of Bachelor's Degrees Awarded by Selected Fields in Historically Black Colleges and Nationally, 1965-66 to 1972-73

	1965-66	1966-67	1967-68	1968-69	1969-70	1970-71	1971-72	1972-73
Biological sciences								
Black colleges	6.7	6.0	6.1	5.7	4.9	4.9	4.2	3.5
National	5.2	5.1	5.0	4.8	4.7	4.3	4.4	4.4
Business and management								
Black colleges	4.9	5.9	7.3	8.9	11.0	13.7	14.0	15.1
National	12.1	12.4	12.6	12.9	13.3	13.8	13.4	13.1
Education								
Black colleges	44.9	43.3	40.2	37.6	36.1	35.1	34.6	33.4
National	22.6	21.5	21.3	20.9	20.9	21.0	15.5	15.4
Physical sciences								
Black colleges	2.6	2.4	2.2	1.9	2.0	1.6	1.7	1.6
National	3.3	3.2	3.1	2.9	2.7	2.5	2.5	2.4
Social sciences								
Black colleges	17.2	18.5	19.4	20.8	22.3	22.6	21.9	19.6
National	17.9	18.6	19.1	19.3	19.4	19.9	19.7	20.2
Other								
Black colleges	23.7	23.9	24.8	25.1	23.8	22.1	23.6	26.8
National	38.9	39.2	38.9	39.2	38.9	38.5	44.5	44.5

Source: Elias Blake, Jr. et al., Degrees Granted and Enrollment Trends in Historically Black Colleges: An Eight-Year Study, Vol. 1, no. 1 (Washington, D.C.: Institute for Services to Education, Inc., October 1974), p. 38.

TABLE 4.6

Bachelor's, Master's, and Doctor's Degrees in
Ethnic Studies Conferred in U.S. Institutions
of Higher Education, 1972–73 and 1973–74

	Total All Degrees	Bachelor's Degrees Requiring Four or Five Years	Master's Degrees	Doctor's Degrees (Ph.D., Ed.D., etc.)
1972–73				
Afro-American (black culture) studies	372	351	21	--
Native American cultural studies	4	4	--	--
Mexican American cultural studies	93	84	9	--
Urban studies	1,561	891	670	7
1973–74				
Afro-American (black culture) studies	414	392	19	3
Native American cultural studies	20	20	--	--
Mexican American cultural studies	123	111	12	--
Urban studies	2,090	1,289	794	7

Source: U.S. Department of Health, Education and Welfare,
"Earned Degrees Conferred, 1972–73 and 1973–74," Summary Data
(Washington, D.C.: U.S. Government Printing Office, 1976),
Table 5.

NATIVE AMERICANS

Native Americans are unique in regard to college outcome and
earned degrees. Many Native American college students are supported by the Bureau of Indian Affairs programs: In 1974 about 24
percent were supported financially by BIA programs; about 24.8
percent (1,141) degrees earned by Native Americans were earned

by students enrolled in those programs; while 75.2 percent (3,457) of all other degrees were earned by students attending schools without the support of the BIA (see Table 4.7). Many Native American students outside of the BIA programs attend the one and only historically Native American college, Pembroke State College in North Carolina. A large portion of these students are Lukbee Indians of North Carolina, whose ancestors refused to leave their homes in North Carolina and go West to the reservation and therefore lost their right to benefits from the BIA-sponsored programs (Dian and Eliades 1972).

TABLE 4.7

Enrollment and Educational Attainment, Bureau of
Indian Affairs Higher Education Programs,
1973 and 1974

	1973	1974	Percent Change
Total enrollment	13,558	13,895	+2.5
Undergraduate enrollment	13,069	13,374	+2.3
Graduate enrollment	489	521	+6.5
Bachelor's degrees earned	770	1,141	+48.2
Graduate degrees earned	168	226	+34.5

Sources: U.S. Department of Interior, Bureau of Indian Affairs, Office of Indian Education Programs, Fiscal Year 1973 Statistics Concerning Indian Education and Fiscal Year 1974 Statistics Concerning Indian Education (Washington, D.C.: U.S. Government Printing Office, 1974, 1975).

HISPANIC AMERICANS

Data on Hispanic American college graduates suggest that only half of the percentage of Hispanic Americans who are enrolled in college eventually earn degrees. As stated earlier, this may be a result of Mexican American dominance in the Southwestern states where two-year colleges are popular; and of Puerto Rican Americans who are located mainly in New York City with its historically poor elementary and secondary schools for minorities. Further programmatic efforts by colleges to deal with the bilinguial and bicultural needs of Hispanic American college students have been inadequate.

ASIAN AMERICANS

Asian Americans, based upon their percentage of college enrollment and the percentage who earn degrees, appear to be holding their own. However, we feel that there is an underrepresentation of Asian Americans who earn degrees, based upon the high percentage of Asian Americans who graduate from high school and the high percentage of those who graduate in the upper half of their graduating class.

It is suggested that programs designed for Asian American children and young adults be planned with their culture foremost in mind and developed and implemented by members of those ethnic groups. It is evident from the increased immigration of Asian Americans to this country since 1965 that colleges and universities should expect a sizable Asian student population, along with unique needs related to their language and culture.

5

ENGINEERING
AND PHARMACY

Within higher education, engineering is the major applied physical science discipline, followed by pharmacy. Both engineering and pharmacy require students to be skilled in the basic physical sciences and mathematics, and such skills are a reflection of the capability of elementary and secondary schools to equip minority students for careers in the "hard" sciences.

ENGINEERING

In 1973 the only minority group considered to be fairly represented in engineering was Asian Americans (see Table 5.1). At the undergraduate level they constituted 2.0 percent of the full time engineering student enrollment, blacks 3.0 percent, Hispanic Americans 3.3 percent, and Native Americans 0.2 percent. (Their representations in the total population are: Asians 0.8 percent, blacks 11.1 percent, Hispanic Americans 4.6 percent, and Native Americans 0.4 percent.)

At the graduate level, the percentage of blacks and Hispanic and Native American engineering enrollment decreased markedly, both for master's-level students and doctoral-level students (see Table 5.2). However, the Asian American student percentage enrollment increased at the graduate level.

Most minority students enrolled in engineering majored in the basic engineering curricula such as chemical, civil, computer, electrical, and general engineering. Few minorities majored in agricultural, architectural, biomedical, ceramic, mining, or petroleum engineering (see Tables 5.3, 5.4, and 5.5). These preferences for particular curricula may be due in part to the

TABLE 5.1

Number and Percent of Minorities Enrolled in Engineering
by Degree Level, Fall 1973

	Bachelor's Degree						Master's Degree		Doctor's Degree	
	First Year	Second Year	Third Year	Fourth and Fifth Year	Full Time	Part Time	Full Time	Part Time	Full Time	Part Time
Hispanic American	1,543	1,269	1,184	2,084	6,080	389	257	254	51	18
Percent	3.0	3.1	2.8	4.0	3.3	2.5	1.1	1.2	0.4	0.4
Native American	93	88	90	111	382	17	35	16	7	2
Percent	0.2	0.2	0.2	0.2	0.2	0.1	0.2	0.1	0.4	--
Asian American	896	757	933	1,233	3,819	359	639	709	303	144
Percent	1.7	1.9	2.2	2.3	2.0	2.3	2.8	3.2	2.5	3.4
Black	2,106	1,319	1,071	1,032	5,528	295	536	222	66	17
Percent	4.1	3.2	2.6	2.0	3.0	1.9	2.4	1.0	0.6	0.4
U.S. total	51,925	40,519	41,673	52,588	186,705	15,692	22,588	21,939	11,904	4,175

Source: Engineering Manpower Commission, Engineers Joint Council, Engineering and Technology Enrollments, Series 1969–73, and follow-up survey, August 1974.

historical background of most minorities in the United States. Minority students have had limited access and little acquaintance with the professions relating to agricultural, geological, and petroleum engineering, because these fields suggest that minorities should return in some fashion back to the farms or the mines, or to spend time surveying petroleum fields in Oklahoma, Texas, and New Mexico. Therefore, given the background of most minorities in this country, the idea of returning to the farm, to the mines, or to the oil fields would be enough to steer many minorities away from such fields.

TABLE 5.2

Enrollment of Blacks in Engineering by
Degree Level, 1969-70 to 1973-74

	1969-70*	1970-71	1971-72	1972-73	1973-74
Bachelor's Degree					
First year	977	1,424	1,289	1,477	2,106
Second year	704	811	926	965	1,319
Third year	430	664	693	838	1,071
Fourth year	397	575	588	661	}1,032
Fifth Year	25	24	26	34	
Full time	2,757	3,753	4,136	4,356	5,528
Part time	168	354	349	491	295
Master's Degree					
Full time	55	106	112	165	536
Part time	84	109	140	172	222
Doctor's Degree					
Full time	22	44	44	49	66
Part time	4	8	13	9	17
Total Graduate Students					
Full time	81	171	192	238	602
Part time	88	119	154	181	239

*Totals for women and minority groups include only numbers actually reported. The totals would be higher if all institutions had reported all categories.

Source: Engineering Manpower Commission, Engineers Joint Council, Engineering and Technology Enrollments, Series 1969-73 and follow-up survey, August 1974.

TABLE 5.3

Bachelor's Degrees in Engineering by Curriculum and Minority Status, 1974

Curriculum	Number of Degrees	Blacks	Hispanic Americans	Asian Americans	Native Americans	Foreign
Aerospace	1,041	13	17	11	0	42
Agricultural	450	0	2	2	0	4
Architectural	320	23	11	6	0	15
Biomedical	174	7	1	2	0	3
Ceramic	156	0	0	1	0	0
Chemical	3,523	29	39	60	5	317
Civil	8,176	96	131	180	10	375
Computer	727	10	7	11	0	36
Electrical	11,347	265	176	347	3	824
Engineering general	1,716	46	62	100	2	118
Engineering sciences	950	14	11	4	0	17
Environmental	129	1	1	2	0	2
Geological	200	1	1	3	0	11
Industrial	2,510	76	45	36	2	157
Marine/Naval	568	2	3	3	1	10
Materials/Metallurgy	580	1	8	6	0	19
Mechanical	7,612	154	106	170	6	403
Mining	260	0	1	3	1	10
Nuclear	339	1	2	4	1	23
Petroleum	299	2	5	2	1	30
Systems	153	0	5	4	0	4
Other engineering	177	2	2	0	0	16
Total	41,407	743	636	957	32	2,436

Source: Engineering Manpower Commission, Engineers Joint Council, Engineering and Technology Degrees 1974, January 1975.

TABLE 5.4

Master's Degrees in Engineering by Curriculum and Minority Status, 1974

Curriculum	Number of Degrees	Blacks	Hispanic Americans	Asian Americans	Native Americans	Foreign
Aerospace	554	4	5	11	0	88
Agricultural	144	1	1	2	0	39
Architectural	30	0	1	2	0	5
Biomedical	127	2	0	3	0	23
Ceramic	46	0	0	0	0	7
Chemical	1,053	6	11	38	0	281
Civil	2,681	18	43	73	2	571
Computer	723	20	3	12	0	117
Electrical	3,702	36	46	122	0	731
Engineering general	626	23	13	48	0	143
Engineering sciences	576	2	4	7	0	83
Environmental	577	1	4	4	0	40
Geological	81	0	0	1	0	14
Industrial	1,502	9	21	18	2	221
Marine/Naval	160	0	0	1	0	36
Materials/Metallurgy	402	2	1	2	0	107
Mechanical	1,999	15	20	62	0	387
Mining	46	0	0	0	0	13
Nuclear	391	6	5	10	0	47
Petroleum	60	0	0	0	0	24
Systems	353	7	7	8	0	93
Other Engineering	52	1	1	1	0	29
Total	15,885	153	186	425	4	3,099

Source: Engineering Manpower Commission, Engineers Joint Council, Engineering and Technology Degrees 1974, January 1975.

TABLE 5.5

Doctoral Degrees in Engineering by Curriculum and Minority Status, 1974

Curriculum	Number of Degrees	Blacks	Hispanic Americans	Asian Americans	Native Americans	Foreign
Aerospace	168	0	0	6	0	42
Agricultural	51	0	0	1	0	24
Architectural	0	0	0	0	0	0
Biomedical	36	0	0	0	0	4
Ceramic	17	0	0	0	0	3
Chemical	403	1	3	9	0	147
Civil	393	2	4	14	0	144
Computer	83	0	0	1	0	16
Electrical	700	3	1	25	0	199
Engineering general	136	0	2	10	0	30
Engineering sciences	279	1	0	8	0	76
Environmental	61	1	1	1	0	12
Geological	26	0	0	0	0	9
Industrial	119	1	2	3	0	34
Marine/Naval	18	0	0	1	0	2
Materials/Metallurgy	220	0	2	5	0	70
Mechanical	446	1	2	20	0	130
Mining	8	0	0	0	0	5
Nuclear	100	1	2	1	0	24
Petroleum	19	0	0	0	0	13
Systems	60	0	0	1	0	20
Other Engineering	19	1	1	0	0	10
Total	3,362	12	20	106	0	1,014

Source: Engineering Manpower Commission, Engineers Joint Council, Engineering and Technology Degrees 1974, January 1975.

TABLE 5.6

Engineering Degrees Granted to Minorities by Degree Level, 1972–73 and 1973–74

	Bachelor's Degree			Master's Degree			Doctor's Degree		
	Total	Minority	Percent Minority	Total	Minority	Percent Minority	Total	Minority	Percent Minority
Hispanic Americans									
1972–73	43,429	866	1.99	17,152	139	0.81	3,587	12	0.33
1973–74	41,407	1,037	2.50	15,885	193	1.27	3,362	19	0.56
Asian Americans									
1972–73	43,429	684	1.57	17,152	261	1.52	3,587	55	1.53
1973–74	41,407	958	2.31	15,885	421	2.65	3,362	106	3.15
Native Americans									
1972–73	42,429	46	0.10	17,152	15	0.09	3,587	1	0.03
1973–74	41,407	31	0.07	15,885	4	0.02	3,362	0	--
Blacks									
1972–73	43,429	574	1.00	17,152	83	0.48	3,587	12	0.33
1973–74	41,407	756	1.83	15,885	158	0.99	3,362	12	0.36

Source: Engineering Manpower Commission, Engineers Joint Council, Engineering and Technology Graduates, 1969 through 1974 series and follow-up survey, July 1974.

TABLE 5.7

Class Standing of Minority Engineering Students at 148 Schools by Sex, Fall 1973

Class Standing	Group						Total
	Black	Hispanic American	Asian American	Native American	Other	Caucasian	
Top third							
Men	53	92	139	10	37	0	331
Women	1	5	15	1	22	242	286
Middle third							
Men	91	112	114	19	20	0	356
Women	8	11	2	0	13	165	199
Lower third							
Men	160	161	102	17	16	0	456
Women	12	1	5	0	6	99	123
Not given							
Men	291	125	231	20	111	0	778
Women	18	7	19	0	167	426	637
Total							
Men	595	490	586	66	184	0	1,921
Women	39	24	41	1	208	932	1,245

Note: 134 engineering colleges and 14 technology institutions provided information for this survey. The numbers do not represent U.S. totals in any category.

Source: Engineering Manpower Commission, Engineers Joint Council, Statistics on Women and Minority Students in Engineering, April 1974.

TABLE 5.8

Estimated Enrollment and B.S. Degrees in Engineering Earned
at U.S. Black Colleges and Universities, 1972-73

	Enrollment	Degrees Earned
Prairie View Agricultural and Mechanical College	332	55
Howard University	261	35
Southern University	200	46
North Carolina Agricultural and Technical State University	279	32
Tennessee Agricultural and Industrial State University	217	29
Tuskegee Institute	242	24
Total	1,531	221

Source: Engineering Manpower Commission, Engineering and Technology Degrees, annual report.

TABLE 5.9

Engineering Degrees Granted to Blacks by Degree Level,
1968-69 to 1973-74

	1968-69*	1969-70*	1970-71*	1971-72	1972-73	1973-74
Bachelor's Degrees						
Total	39,972	42,966	43,167	44,190	43,429	41,407
Black	314	378	407	579	657	756
Percent black	0.79	0.88	0.94	1.31	1.51	1.83
Master's Degrees						
Total	14,980	15,548	16,383	17,356	17,152	15,885
Black	17	50	47	78	104	158
Percent black	0.11	0.32	0.29	0.45	0.61	0.99
Doctorates						
Total	3,387	3,620	3,640	3,774	3,587	3,362
Black	2	1	8	13	13	12
Percent black	0.06	0.03	0.22	0.34	0.36	0.36

*Totals for blacks and other minority groups in these years include only numbers actually reported. The totals would be higher if all institutions had reported all categories.

Source: Engineering Manpower Commission, Engineers Joint Council, Engineering and Technology Graduates, 1969 through 1974 series and follow-up survey, July 1974.

In terms of output and earned degrees in engineering (see Tables 5.3, 5.4, and 5.5) in 1974, Hispanic Americans earned 636 bachelor's degrees, 186 master's degrees, and 20 doctoral degrees; Asian Americans earned 957 bachelor's degrees, 425 master's degrees, and 106 doctoral degrees; Native Americans earned 32 bachelor's degrees, 4 master's degrees, and no doctoral degrees; and blacks earned 743 bachelor's degrees, 153 master's degrees, and 12 doctoral degrees (see also Table 5.6).

When we view the data on the number of minorities enrolled in their fourth and fifth year of study we find that the data on earned degrees and enrollment for Hispanic Americans and blacks are somewhat compatible; but when we look at the data on Asian and Native Americans we find that the data are not compatible. For example, in 1973 the percentage of Hispanic American college students enrolled in their fourth year was 4.0 percent compared to only 2.5 percent who earned degrees during that same year. The percentage of Native Americans enrolled in their fourth year in 1973 was 0.2 percent but only 0.07 percent earned degrees during that same year. However, there is no reason for alarm here since the earned degree data is for the year 1973 while the enrollment data is for fall of 1973. It is expected that a larger percent of Hispanic and Native Americans will earn degrees in 1974--if not, there may be a cause for alarm.

There is some evidence that minority students are having some difficulties with their studies in engineering, because a disproportionate number of them are ranked in the lower third of their classes academically (see Table 5.7). It is clear that many minorities attend poor schools that offer a poor background in mathematics.

PHARMACY

Minorities enrolled in pharmacy are also of interest to us because of this field's relationship to the "hard" sciences. In 1972 an estimated 18,000 students were enrolled in pharmacy; among these 659 were blacks, 254 Hispanic Americans, 29 Native Americans, and 672 Asian Americans. The total minority enrollment constituted 9.0 percent, or 1,661 students (see Table 5.10).

It should be noted that out of the 659 black students enrolled in pharmacy, almost half (372) were enrolled in historically black colleges. The black pharmacy schools are located at Howard University, Texas Southern University, Xavier University, and Florida Agricultural and Mechanical University.

In 1974 the listing of all minorities who were practicing engineers in the United States reveals that percentagewise few are

TABLE 5.10

Estimates of Pharmacy Enrollment by
Race and Ethnicity, 1972-73

Race	Number	Percent	Enrolled in Black Colleges	Percent
Black	659	3.6	372	2.0
Hispanic American	254	1.4	--	--
Native American	29	0.2	--	--
Asian American	672	3.6	--	--
Total minority	1,661	9.0	--	--
Total	18,500	100.0	372	2.0

Note: Approximately 56 percent of all black pharmacy students are enrolled at Howard, Texas Southern, Xavier, and Florida Agricultural and Mechanical universities.

Source: American Association of Colleges of Pharmacy, Report on Enrollment in Schools and Colleges of Pharmacy, 1972-73, 1974.

TABLE 5.11

Minorities Employed in Engineering, 1974

	Number in Engineering Occupation	Number with Engineering Degrees	Percent in U.S. Population	Percent in Engineering Occupation
Black	14,800	8,100	11.1	1.2
Hispanic American	20,000	15,000	4.4	1.6
Native American	6,800	5,500	0.39	0.2
Japanese	5,200	4,400	0.29	0.42
Chinese	7,800	6,600	0.21	0.63
Filipino	6,200	5,300	0.17	0.50
Other minorities	16,700	14,200	0.35	1.34

Source: Population statistics are from 1970 Census data in Statistical Abstract of the United States, 1972. Engineering figures were abstracted from data provided by the National Center for Educational Statistics, U.S. Department of Health, Education and Welfare.

TABLE 5.12

Racial/Ethnic Groups Identified in the Comprehensive Roster of Doctoral Scientists and Engineers, by Academic Year of Doctorate

Period of Ph.D. Graduation	All Minorities		Racial/Ethnic Group					U.S. Total
	Number	Percent	Black	Asian	Latin	American	Other	
1930–34	89	1.7	18	59	12	0	0	5,750
1935–39	110	1.5	39	49	22	0	0	7,335
1940–44	189	2.2	51	100	36	0	0	8,768
1945–49	441	4.5	118	234	73	0	16	9,889
1950–54	886	3.5	156	612	95	12	11	25,482
1955–59	1,265	4.5	270	829	111	18	32	27,909
1960–64	2,582	6.5	257	2,007	253	21	44	39,423
1965–69	5,365	8.0	508	4,275	431	30	121	66,795
1970–72	3,736	7.0*	443	2,822	374	25	72	53,478
Total	14,663	6.0	1,860	10,987	1,412	106	298	244,829

*This decline from 1965–69 was probably attributable to poorer coverage of foreign doctoral recipients in the 1970–72 cohort.

Source: National Research Council, National Academy of Sciences, "Summary Report 1973 Doctorate Recipients from United States Universities," May 1974.

black, Hispanic, or Native Americans. This is not true, however, for Asian Americans (see Table 5.11).

This trend among the "hard" sciences and minority student enrollment in the United States is also reflected in the number and percentage of minorities who have received doctorates in this country since 1930: from a total of 244,829 doctorates awarded in science and engineering, 1,860 went to blacks, 10,987 to Asian Americans, 1,412 to Hispanic Americans, and 106 to Native Americans (see Table 5.12).

6

GRADUATE AND
PROFESSIONAL SCHOOL
ENROLLMENT
AND EARNED DEGREES

Graduate education in the United States is an area in which minorities will have to increase their numbers if they are to move into the top echelon of their professions. Enrollment in graduate schools generally leads toward a master's degree, a doctorate, or a professional degree such as law, dentistry, or medicine.

As we move up the hierarchy within institutions of higher education in the United States--from the lower division of undergraduate schools, to the upper division of undergraduate schools, to graduate school--we find that the percentage of minorities enrolled tends to decrease as we move up the hierarchy. While we may have a few problems in clearly defining the minority availability pool for undergraduate education, we have less difficulty in defining the availability pool for graduate studies. Two criteria seem to hold for graduate students: applicants must have the money and motivation to matriculate, and the applicants must have the necessary academic credentials to gain admittance to graduate studies. The first criterion may result in reduced minority enrollment in graduate schools because past histories would suggest that minorities have not been encouraged to do graduate studies and, generally, minorities have fewer financial resources needed to pursue graduate studies. The second criterion involves academic qualifications for admittance to graduate schools which may result in reduced minority enrollment because a disproportionate number of minorities are found in the academic bottom half of their graduating class. (This generalization may not apply to black students because about 50 percent of all black college graduates attend historically black colleges.)

Many minority students who attend undergraduate schools are supported by equal opportunity programs, which in itself indicates that many of these are ill-prepared from high school for college-level work. Therefore, it seems fair to assume that some students

TABLE 6.1

Estimates of Graduate Enrollment in U.S. Institutions of Higher Education,
except Law, Dental, and Medical, 1968, 1970, 1972, and 1974

Year	Native American	Black	Asian American	Hispanic American	White	Total
1968-69	1,908	30,130	7,752	7,313	837,897	885,000
Percent	0.2	3.4	0.9	0.8	94.7	100.0
1970-71	3,049	42,634	18,169	11,902	955,246	1,031,000
Percent	0.3	4.1	1.8	1.2	92.7	100.0
1972-73	3,807	54,484	19,623	15,432	972,704	1,066,000
Percent	0.4	5.1	1.8	1.4	91.2	100.0
1974-75	3,906	63,475	19,414	18,405	1,084,798	1,190,000
Percent	0.3	5.3	1.6	1.5	91.2	100.0

Sources: U.S. Department of Health, Education and Welfare, Projections of Education Statistics to 1984-85, and Office for Civil Rights, "Racial and Ethnic Enrollment Data from Institutions of Higher Education, Fall 1970," 1972.

TABLE 6.2

Graduate School Full- and Part-Time Enrollment
by Field of Study for Various Ethnic Groups
(percentage)

Field and Source	Whites[a]	Blacks	Native Americans	Asian Americans	Hispanic Americans
Business					
ETS[b]	95.8	2.2	.3	.9	.8
ACE[c]		1.0		3.0	
Education					
ETS	91.6	5.6	.5	.7	1.6
ACE		4.6		.7	
Engineering					
ETS	96.8	.9	.1	1.6	.6
ACE		1.1		10.0	
Arts and humanities					
ETS	95.2	2.3	.2	1.0	1.3
ACE		1.3		1.5	
Social sciences					
ETS	92.6	5.0	.3	1.0	1.1
ACE		2.6		2.4	
Biological sciences					
ETS	96.0	1.8	.3	1.1	.8
ACE		1.4		1.8	
Physical sciences					
ETS	95.6	2.1	.8	1.0	.5
ACE		1.3		6.7	

[a]White totals were obtained by subtracting minority totals from 100 percent.

[b]Educational Testing Service.

[c]American Council on Education.

Sources: Bruce Hamilton, Graduate School Programs for Minority/Disadvantaged Students, Report of an Initial Survey (Princeton, N.J.: Educational Testing Service, 1973); John A. Creager, The American Graduate Student: A Normative Description, American Council on Education Research Reports 6, no. 5 (October 1971).

TABLE 6.3

Comparison of Data Sources on 1970 Graduate School
Enrollment in the United States, except Law,
Dental, and Medical
(percentages)

Source	Blacks	Asian Americans	Hispanic Americans	Native Americans	Other
Office for Civil Rights, 1970	4.2	1.9	1.2	0.3	92.3
American Council on Education	2.3	3.8	--	--	93.9
Educational Testing Service	3.3	0.8	1.0	0.3	94.6
U.S. Census	3.1	1.7	0.5	0.1	93.9

Sources: U.S. Department of Health, Education and Welfare, Office for Civil Rights, "Racial and Ethnic Data From Institutions of Higher Education, Fall 1970," 1972; John A. Creager, The American Graduate Student: A Normative Description, American Council on Education Research Reports 6, no. 5 (October 1971); Bruce Hamilton, Graduate School Programs for Minority/Disadvantaged Students, Report of an Initial Survey (Princeton, N.J.: Educational Testing Service, 1973); U.S. Bureau of the Census, Characteristics of the Population, 1970.

TABLE 6.4

Total Family Income of First-Year Graduate Students

Family Income	Percent of Graduate Students Enrolled
Less than $5,000	24.3
$5,000-$11,999	43.7
$12,000 and over	32.0

Source: John A. Creager, The American Graduate Student: A Normative Description, American Council on Education Research Reports 6, no. 5 (October 1971).

who are able to overcome those deficiencies (and many do) must find
it difficult to end up in the top half of their graduating class. It is
generally those students who end up in the top half of their graduating
classes who find it possible to gain entrance into graduate school.
Further, affirmative action efforts to admit minority students to
graduate school, such as equal opportunity programs, have, by and
large, not surfaced at the graduate level.

GRADUATE ENROLLMENT (EXCEPT DENTAL, MEDICAL, AND LAW)

In 1974 the minority graduate enrollment in institutions of
higher education was 3,906 Native Americans for 0.3 percent of the
total graduate student enrollment; 63,475 blacks for 5.3 percent;
19,414 Asian Americans for 1.6 percent; and 18,405 Hispanic Americans for 1.5 percent (see Table 6.1). The only group that came
close to equaling their representation in the total population (0.8
percent) was Asian Americans. However, this is not a case of overrepresentation but underrepresentation based upon the high number
and percentage of Asian American students who graduate from undergraduate programs and who have a high representation of enrollment
in prestigious colleges and universities. Graduate enrollment prior
to 1974 show a similar trend (see Tables 6.1, 6.2, and 6.3).

Although it may appear that Native Americans have reached
parity in the percent of students enrolled in graduate programs, the
authors cannot agree with such an assumption. While the total
Native American population in the country is 0.4 percent and their
representation in graduate school is also 0.4 percent, as mentioned
before, we find it difficult to agree with the Census Bureau figures
on the actual number of Native Americans in this country. The data
are more alarming when one considers the high suicide rate, high
death rate, and low life expectancy for the Native American population. The data cannot be explained by an increase in the population
by natural means such as increased birth rate, decreased death rate,
or a combination of the two which results in lengthening the life expectancy of the Native American. The number of Native Americans
in the United States is probably much higher.

DENTAL SCHOOLS

Dental schools, at least for minorities, have not been as at-
tractive as medical schools. During the 1974-75 school year the
numbers of minorities enrolled in U.S. dental schools were 945
blacks for 4.7 percent of the total dental school enrollment; 15 Puerto

TABLE 6.5

Dental School Minority Enrollment
(percentages in parentheses)

Year	Black	Puerto Rican	Mexican American	Native American	Asian American	Other Minority
First year						
1972-73	266 (5.0)	3 (.1)	53 (1.0)	5 (.1)	138 (2.6)	10 (.2)
1974-75	279 (5.0)	7 (.1)	68 (1.2)	12 (.2)	142 (2.5)	43 (.8)
Second year						
1972-73	235 (5.0)	5 (.1)	30 (.6)	4 (.1)	108 (2.3)	17 (.4)
1974-75	242 (4.5)	4 (.1)	64 (1.2)	12 (.2)	131 (2.4)	33 (.6)
Third year						
1972-73	149 (3.4)	2 (.0)	23 (.5)	4 (.1)	92 (2.1)	11 (.3)
1974-75	227 (4.8)	2 (.0)	45 (.9)	5 (.1)	133 (2.8)	17 (.4)
Fourth year						
1972-73	115 (2.9)	3 (.3)	13 (.3)	1 (.0)	71 (1.8)	13 (.3)
1974-75	197 (4.5)	2 (.0)	33 (.8)	4 (.1)	107 (2.4)	14 (.3)
Total						
1972-73	765 (4.2)	13 (.1)	119 (.7)	14 (.1)	409 (2.2)	51 (.3)
1974-75	945 (4.7)	15 (.1)	210 (1.)	33 (.2)	513 (2.5)	107 (.5)

Sources: American Dental Association, Annual Report 1972-73 Dental Education Supplement, "Minority Student Enrollment and Opportunities in U.S. Dental Schools," and Annual Report 1974-75 Dental Education Supplement No. 4, "Minority Report."

TABLE 6.6

Enrollment in Black Dental Schools in the United States, 1972-73

School and Year	Total	Blacks	Percent	Black Graduates	Percent
Meharry					
1972-73	162	136	19.2	26	35.1
1974-75	168	150		27	17.5
Howard					
1972-73	367	261	36.8	33	44.6
1974-75	382	308		48	31.2
Total					
1972-73	--	709	100.0	74	100.0
1974-75	--	945	100.0	154	100.0

Sources: American Dental Association, Annual Report 1972-73 Dental Education Supplement, "Minority Student Enrollment and Opportunities in U.S. Dental Schools"; and the 1974-75 "Minority Report."

Ricans for 0.1 percent; 210 Mexican Americans for 1.0 percent; 33
Native Americans for 0.2 percent; 518 Asian Americans for 2.5 percent; and 107 other minority individuals for 0.5 percent (see Table
6.5). As the data indicate, the actual number of minorities enrolled
in dental schools is low. In that same school year 154 black Americans received degrees from dental schools for 3.4 percent of the
total number of degrees awarded; no individual of Puerto Rican
descent received a degree in dentistry during that year; 31 Mexican
Americans for 0.7 percent; 2 Native Americans for 0.001 percent;
113 Asian Americans for 2.5 percent; and 35 other minority individuals for 0.8 percent.

The immediate future appears bleak for Puerto Ricans and
Native Americans based upon enrollment in their fourth year in dental
school during the 1974-75 school year. During that year only two
Puerto Rican students and four Native Americans had reached their
fourth year of dental studies. However, there is no guarantee that
the students who have reached their fourth year will graduate. Therefore, it is possible that the 1975 school graduation class will find no
Puerto Ricans or Native Americans.

The black dental school enrollment and graduation is slightly
different from that of other minority groups because many black
students are enrolled in historically black dental schools: Meharry
Medical College in Nashville, Tennessee, and Howard University
Dental College in Washington, D.C. In 1974, 458 black dental students were enrolled in either Meharry and Howard, which constituted
48.5 percent of all black dental students (see Table 6.6). The remain-
ing black dental students were enrolled at integrated or predominantly
white dental schools. In 1974, out of the 154 black dental students
who graduated, 75 were graduated from Meharry and Howard, schools
which constituted 48.7 percent of all black dental school graduates.

MEDICAL SCHOOLS

The percentage of minority students enrolled in medical schools
was slightly higher than that enrolled in dental, law, and other professional schools. It should be noted that data compiled by the American Medical Association and the Association of Medical Colleges does
not always present similar data on Asian Americans. However,
comprehensive data are presented for blacks, Native Americans,
Mexican Americans, and mainland Puerto Ricans. In 1974, 3,045
blacks enrolled in medical schools, constituting 6 percent of the total
medical school enrollment; 97 Native Americans for 0.2 percent; 913
Asian Americans for 1.8 percent; 496 Mexican Americans for 1.1
percent; and 123 Puerto Ricans for 0.2 percent (see Table 6.7).

TABLE 6.7

Total Minority Enrollment in U.S. Medical
Schools, 1969-73

	1969-70	1970-71	1971-72	1972-73	1973-74
Black[a]					
Number	1,042	1,509	2,055	2,582	3,045
Percent	2.8	3.6	4.7	5.5	6.0
Native American					
Number	18	18	42	69	97
Percent	--	--	.1	.1	.2
Mexican American					
Number	92	148	252	361	496
Percent	0.2	0.4	0.6	.8	1.1
Asian American[b]					
Number	490	--	738	--	913
Percent	.13	--	1.69	--	1.8
Mainland Puerto Rican					
Number	26	48	76	90	123
Percent	.1	.1	.2	.2	.2
Total enrollment	37,690	40,238	43,650	47,259	50,716

Note: These figures include only U.S. citizens.

[a]In 1969, 1.2 percent of all black medical students were enrolled in Howard and Meharry Medical Colleges; in 1973-74 the percent was still 1.2; in 1970-71 it was 1.1 percent; in 1971-72, 1.2 percent. In 1968 these two schools enrolled 63 percent of all black
medical students, 27 percent in 1971; they graduated 87 percent of
all M.D.s in 1968 and 57 percent in 1971.

[b]Competed data on Asian Americans could not be obtained.

Source: Association of American Medical Colleges, Datagram
(Washington, D.C.: 1974).

In 1974, 511 black Americans graduated from medical schools,
79 Mexican Americans, 3 Native Americans, 19 mainland Puerto
Ricans, which constituted 4.5 percent, 0.7 percent, 0.03 percent,
and 0.2 percent for each group, respectively (see Tables 6.8 and
6.9). The total number of minorities graduating from U.S. medical
schools in 1974 was 612 or 5.4 percent of the graduating class.

Again, it must be noted that these percentages of graduates do not
include Asian Americans as they are not listed as minorities by the
American Medical Association for data-collection purposes. Data
are not available on the number who graduated during the 1974 school
year.

It should be noted that a sizable number of black medical students are enrolled in the two historically black medical colleges,
Meharry Medical College and Howard University Medical College.

TABLE 6.8

Percentage Minority Enrollment in U.S. Medical Schools,
1972-73 and 1973-74

	1972-73		1973-74[a]	
	Number	Percent	Number	Percent
First year enrollment[b]				
Black	858	6.4	870	6.4
Mexican American	151	1.1	170	1.2
Native American	33	0.2	33	0.2
Puerto Rican (mainland)[c]	44	0.3	48	0.3
Four-group total	1,086	8.1	1,121	8.2
Graduates				
Black	341	3.3	511	4.5
Mexican American	39	0.4	79	0.7
Native American	8	0.08	3	0.03
Puerto Rican (mainland)[c]	10	0.1	19	0.2
Four-group total	398	3.8	612	5.4
Total enrollment				
Black	2,593	5.5	2,961	5.9
Mexican American	380	0.8	512	1.0
Native American	68	0.1	93	0.2
Puerto Rican (mainland)[c]	98	0.2	140	0.3
Four-group total	3,139	6.6	3,706	7.4

[a]Harvard did not report data.
[b]First-year enrollment data exclude repeaters from the count.
[c]University of Puerto Rico excluded from count.
Source: Journal of the American Medical Association 231
(January 1975).

TABLE 6.9

Black U.S. Citizens Serving in Medical Residencies,
by Specialty, as of September 1, 1973

Specialty	U.S. and Canadian Graduates Total	Foreign Graduates Total	Total All Graduates
Anesthesiology	7	31	38
Child psychiatry	3	1	4
Diagnostic radiology	9		9
Dermatology	10	2	12
Family practice	51	4	55
General surgery	110	24	134
Internal medicine	136	36	172
Neurological surgery	13	2	15
Neurology	10	17	27
Nuclear medicine	1	1	2
Obstetrics-gynecology	116	27	143
Ophthalmology	27	5	32
Orthopedic surgery	34	5	39
Otolaryngology	11	3	14
Pathology	17	18	35
Pediatrics	70	21	91
Pediatric allergy	1	1	2
Pediatric cardiology	5	1	6
Physical medicine and rehabilitation	3	6	9
Plastic surgery	1	2	3
Psychiatry	58	20	78
Radiology	39	12	51
Therapeutic radiology	2	1	3
Thoracic surgery	3	5	8
Urology	21	10	31
Other specialties	11	8	19
Total	769	263	1,032

Source: Journal of the American Medical Association, Supplement, Vol. 231 (January 1975).

It should also be noted that the retention rate for minority medical students is quite high. For example, out of the 810 black students admitted in 1972, 716 were retained as of June 1974; 31 Native Americans admitted and 30 retained; 138 Mexican Americans admitted and 133 retained; and 37 mainland Puerto Ricans admitted and 34 retained (see Table 6.10). However, there is some evidence that a larger percentage of minority students have to repeat at least one year. In 1973, 5.2 percent of the black students were asked to repeat at least a year; 5.4 percent of Mexican American students, and 4.0 percent of Puerto Rican students, compared to 0.6 percent for all other students (see Table 6.11).

TABLE 6.10

Students Admitted 1971-72 to 1973-74 and
Still in School in June 1974

	Black	Native American	Mexican American	Puerto Rican (Mainland)	All Students
Admitted 1971-72	758	21	117	33	10,962
Retained June 1974					
Number	649	21	110	30	10,500
Percent	86	100	94	91	96
Admitted 1972-73	810	31	138	37	12,520
Retained June 1974					
Number	716	30	133	34	12,118
Percent	88	97	96	92	97
Admitted 1973-74	864	37	169	48	13,062
Retained June 1974					
Number	802	37	166	47	12,842
Percent	93	100	98	98	98

Source: Journal of the American Medical Association, Supplement, Vol. 231 (January 1975).

TABLE 6.11

Students Repeating the Academic Year, 1973-74

	Black	Native American	Mexican American	Puerto Rican (Mainland)	All Other Students
First-Year Class					
Enrolled total	995	41	178	56	12,642
Repeating					
Number	120	8	8	8	142
Percent	12.1	19.5	4.5	14.2	1.1
All Other Classes					
Enrolled total	1,966	52	334	126	33,477
Repeating					
Number	102	3	18	5	202
Percent	5.2	5.8	5.4	4.0	0.6

Source: Journal of the American Medical Association, Supplement, Vol. 231 (January 1975).

While the minority enrollment percentage has remained nearly constant over the last several years, the percentage of graduates has increased slightly. In 1972 the total minority enrollment in medical schools was 8.1 percent compared to 8.2 percent in 1973; however, in 1972 the number of minority students receiving medical degrees was 3.8 percent compared to 5.4 percent in 1973.

LAW SCHOOLS

Law schools are distinguished from medical and dental schools in that the latter demand basic skills in the biological and physical sciences and in mathematics as compared to a more basic background in the language arts and the social sciences for law school. A successful law school student should have better-than-average language skills. It is probably a good prognosis that an English major would do well in a law school as compared to majors from other disciplines.

It was surprising to find that among the three major professional schools, a smaller percent of minorities was enrolled in law school than in the other schools. In 1974, 4,995 law students were black, which comprised 4.7 percent of all law students; 1,357 were

TABLE 6.12

Minority Students Enrolled in Approved Law Schools, 1969-74

	First Year	Second Year	Third Year	Fourth Year	Year Not Stated	Total
Black						
1974-75	1,910	1,587	1,329	145	24	4,995
1973-74	1,943	1,443	1,207	101	123	4,817
1972-73	1,907	1,324	1,106	74	12	4,423
1971-72	1,716	1,147	761	55	65	3,744
1969-70	1,115	574	395	44	--	2,128
Chicano						
(Mexican American)						
1974-75	559	447	329	17	5	1,357
1973-74	539	386	271	63	0	1,259
1972-73	480	337	238	17	0	1,072
1971-72	403	262	170	11	37	883
1969-70	245	113	54	0	--	412
Puerto Rican						
1974-75	117	87	56	3	0	263
1973-74	96	47	32	5	0	180
1972-73	73	40	25	5	0	143
1971-72	49	25	18	2	0	94
1969-70	29	14	13	5	--	61
Other Hispanic						
American						
1974-75	182	92	97	11	5	387
1973-74	94	70	59	4	34	261
1972-73	96	72	60	3	0	231
1971-72	74	62	35	3	5	179
1969-70	35	18	19	3	--	75
Native American						
1974-75	110	90	65	0	0	265
1973-74	109	65	44	3	1	222
1972-73	79	48	44	2	0	173
1971-72	71	46	18	2	3	140
1969-70	44	17	10	1	--	72
Asian American						
1974-75	429	322	288	21	3	1,063
1973-74	327	297	202	19	5	850
1972-73	298	218	144	20	1	681
1971-72	254	142	72	7	5	480
1969-70	84	55	42	4	--	185
Other (group not						
stated)						
1974-75	1	1	1	0	0	3
1973-74	6	5	1	0	0	12
1972-73	1	2	2	2	0	7
1971-72	0	23	25	0	0	48
Total minority-						
group students						
1974-75	3,308	2,626	2,165	197	37	8,333
1973-74	3,114	2,313	1,816	195	163	7,601
1972-73	2,934	2,041	1,619	123	13	6,730
1971-72	2,567	1,707	1,099	80	115	5,568
1969-70	1,552	791	533	57	--	2,933
TOTAL ALL RACES						
1974-75	38,074	34,071	29,800	3,763	--	105,708

Source: American Bar Association, Law Schools and Bar Admission Requirement--A Review of Legal Education in the United States--Fall 1974 (Chicago, 1975).

94

TABLE 6.13

Quartile Ranking after Three Years of Study of Disadvantaged
Law Students Who Started School in 1970

	Top Quartile	Middle Top Quartile	Lower Middle Quartile	Lowest Quartile	Unclassified	Total
Blacks	7	27	63	138	27	262
Chicanos	6	10	18	38	15	87
Hispanic Americans	0	3	4	4	0	11
Asian Americans	5	3	12	9	19	48
Native Americans	1	1	2	7	1	12
Whites	0	0	2	1	0	3
Women	1	1	0	12	0	14

Notes: Total group = 423 (excluding women, since they are included in the other groups), out of the 587 who advanced into the third year in good standing. This figure includes 512 who advanced in good standing from among those in good standing and 75 who advanced in good standing who had been on probation.

Of those in the disadvantaged group who advanced into the third year on probation, and for whom statistics were available and furnished, the table shows the distribution by racial groups; all are in the lowest quartile: blacks 49, Chicanos 14, Hispanic Americans 1, and Asian Americans 8.

Source: American Bar Association, Law Schools and Bar Admission Requirements--A Review of Legal Education in the United States--Fall 1974 (Chicago, 1975).

TABLE 6.14

Academic Status after Three Years of Study of Disadvantaged
Law Students Who Started School in 1970

	Blacks	Chicanos	Hispanic Americans	Asian Americans	Native Americans	Others
In good standing	342	105	3	22	20	60
On probation	101	11	0	5	7	8
Dismissed	87	20	1	5	4	12
Readmitted second year	23	8	0	0	0	3
Readmitted first year	15	1	0	0	0	1
Total identified	568	145	4	32	31	84
Potential total in school second year at start of 1971-72	481	125	3	27	27	72

Source: American Bar Association, Law Schools and Bar Admission Requirements--A Review of Legal Education in the United States--Fall 1974 (Chicago, 1975).

Mexican Americans for 1.3 percent; 263 were mainland Puerto
Ricans for 0.25 percent; 387 were other Hispanic Americans for
0.37 percent; 265 were Native Americans for 0.25 percent; and
1,063 were Asian Americans for 1.0 percent (see Table 6.12).

The most notable increases in minority law school enrollment
between 1969 and 1975 have occurred among Hispanic Americans,
Native Americans, and Asian Americans. In 1969 there were 412
Mexican American law students compared to 1,357 in 1975; 61 Puerto
Rican students compared to 263; 72 Native Americans compared to
265; 85 Asian Americans compared to 1,063. Increases in the black
law school enrollment have been less dramatic: in 1969 there were
2,128 black law students compared to 4,995 in 1975.

Many minority students admitted to law school since 1970 have
been admitted under a variety of programs for the economically and
educationally disadvantaged. A survey by the American Bar Association of 1,041 disadvantaged law students admitted in 1970 after
three years in law school indicated that a disproportionate number
of those students are in the lowest quartile of their class, some have
been placed on probation, while others have been dismissed outright.
However, it must be noted that many of these disadvantaged students
ranked in the top and middle top quartile of their class (see Table
6.13). Among the 1,041 disadvantaged students admitted in 1970,
here is the breakdown three years later: of the 568 black students
admitted, 342 remained in good standing, 101 were placed on probation, and 87 were dismissed; of the 145 Chicano students admitted,
105 remained in good standing, 11 on probation, and 20 dismissed;
of the Asian Americans admitted, 22 were in good standing, 5 on
probation, and 5 dismissed; among the 31 Native Americans admitted, 20 remained in good standing, 7 on probation, and 4 dismissed; while among the 84 white disadvantaged students admitted,
60 remained in good standing, 8 on probation, and 12 dismissed
(see Table 6.14). Among the students who were dismissed but re-
admitted, 38 were black, 9 were Chicano, and 4 were white.

THE ACADEMIC DOCTORATE

The fall 1973 enrollment of minority graduate students in
Ph.D.-granting institutions indicated that black students were enrolled in education, health sciences, and social sciences; Hispanic
Americans were concentrated heavily in arts and humanities, education, and social sciences; Native Americans were highly represented in education, health sciences, and social sciences; while
Asian Americans were heavily represented in engineering, health
professions, life sciences, and mathematics (see Tables 6.15, 6.16,
and 6.17).

TABLE 6.15

Statistical Profile of Persons Receiving Doctoral Degrees, by Field of Study, 1972-73

	Arts and Humanities	Education	Engineering	Life Sciences	Mathematics	Physical Sciences	Professional Fields	Social Sciences	All Fields
Number of Ph.D.s conferred[a]	5,364	7,248	3,338	5,068	1,222	4,016	1,461	5,911	33,727[b]
Sex (percents)									
Men	71.2	75.4	98.7	82.8	90.3	93.6	86.3	79.0	82.0
Women	28.8	24.6	1.3	17.2	9.7	6.4	13.7	21.0	18.0
Racial/ethnic group[c]									
White	87.3	84.9	69.5	78.2	--[d]	478.3	86.6	84.8	81.7
Asian American	1.9	1.6	17.4	9.1	--	411.1	3.0	4.0	6.4
Black	1.7	6.7	1.0	2.4	--	41.0	2.1	1.8	2.7
Hispanic American	1.1	.7	.5	1.2	--	4.8	.4	.5	.8
Other	.7	.9	1.0	.8	--	4.5	.2	.8	.7
No usable response	7.3	5.3	10.7	8.3	--	48.3	7.8	8.1	7.7
Marital status									
Married	68.2	77.5	76.3	74.7	69.8	70.8	77.4	73.0	73.5
Not married	28.1	19.6	21.1	21.9	26.8	26.0	18.2	24.0	23.1
Unknown	3.7	2.8	2.6	3.4	3.4	3.2	4.4	3.0	3.4
Median age at doctorate	32.0	36.5	30.4	30.1	29.1	29.1	33.2	30.5	33.3
Postdoctoral employment									
Educational institution	77.8	74.9	22.6	32.5	65.2	19.7	69.1	59.3	53.7
Industry, business	1.7	1.7	39.7	7.4	9.2	16.1	5.8	4.4	9.0
Government	1.6	8.4	12.8	9.5	6.1	8.9	6.7	11.5	8.3
Nonprofit organization	1.8	3.6	2.5	2.5	.9	1.0	7.5	6.2	3.3
Other and unknown	4.2	4.3	3.9	3.9	3.4	3.3	2.3	4.8	3.9
Postdoctoral status unknown	8.1	4.7	4.4	5.7	6.1	6.9	6.5	5.9	6.1

Note: The classification of degrees by field differs somewhat from that in most publications of the National Center for Education Statistics. The differences are that history is included under arts and sciences rather than social sciences, and psychology is included under social sciences. Because of rounding, percents may not add to 100.0.

[a]Includes Ph.D., Ed.D., and comparable degrees at the doctoral level. Excludes first-professional degrees, such as M.D., D.D.S., and D.V.M.

[b]Includes 99 degrees in other or unspecified fields not shown separately.

[c]Based upon responses from 81 percent of the graduates.

[d]Mathematics is included under physical sciences.

Source: National Academy of Sciences/National Research Council, Summary Report 1973 Doctorate Recipients from U.S. Universities, May 1974.

TABLE 6.16

Field of Doctorate

Racial/Ethnic Group	Physical Sciences	Engineering	Life Sciences	Social Sciences	Arts and Humanities	Professional Fields	Education	Total
White/Caucasian								
Number	3,396	1,902	3,185	4,069	3,894	994	4,811	22,251
H	15.3	8.5	14.3	18.3	17.5	4.4	21.6	
V	78.3	69.5	78.2	84.8	87.3	86.6	84.9	81.7
Black/Negro/Afro-American[a]								
Number	45	27	96	87	74	24	382	735
H	6.1	3.7	13.1	11.8	10.1	3.1	52.0	
V	1.0	1.0	2.4	1.8	1.7	2.1	6.7	2.7
Native American[b]								
Number	10	7	17	21	18	1	34	108
H	9.3	6.5	15.7	19.4	16.7	.9	31.5	
V	.2	.3	.4	.4	.4	.1	.6	.4
Hispanic American (including Mexican American and Chicano designations)[c]								
Number	35	14	49	26	49	4	38	215
H	16.3	6.5	22.8	12.1	22.8	1.9	17.7	
V	.8	.5	1.2	.5	1.1	.4	.7	.8
Puerto Rican American[d]								
Number	3	3	7	8	6		10	37
H	8.1	8.1	18.9	21.6	16.2		27.0	
V	.1	.1	.2	.2	.1		.2	.1

								Total
Asian American[e]								
Number	480	476	372	190	84	36	93	1,731
H	27.7	27.5	21.5	11.0	4.9	2.0	5.4	
V	11.1	17.4	9.1	4.0	1.9	3.0	1.6	6.4
Other								
Number	10	17	7	8	11	1	4	58
H	17.2	29.3	12.1	13.8	19.0	1.7	6.9	
V	.2	.6	.2	.2	.2	.1	.1	.2
No usable response								
Number	359	292	340	387	325	91	298	2,092
H	17.2	14.0	16.3	18.5	15.5	4.2	14.2	
V	8.3	10.7	8.3	8.1	7.3	7.8	5.3	7.7
TOTAL								
Number	4,338	2,738	4,073	4,796	4,461	1,151	5,670	27,227
H	15.9	10.1	15.0	17.6	16.4	4.1	20.8	
V	100.0	100.1	100.0	100.0	100.0	100.1	100.1	100.0

Note: H indicates the horizontal percentages which sum to 100 percent across the doctoral fields for each racial/ethnic group. V indicates the vertical percentages which sum to 100 percent for each doctoral field.

[a]Includes 7 persons who checked this category and one other.
[b]Twenty persons checked only this category; 88 checked Native American and white.
[c]Includes 45 persons who checked this category and white.
[d]Eight persons in this category also checked white.
[e]Twelve persons checked this category and white.

Source: National Academy of Sciences/National Research Council, Summary Report 1973 Doctorate Recipients from U.S. Universities, May 1974.

TABLE 6.17

Enrollment of Minority Graduate Students: Number in Each Field of Study, Fall 1973

Field of Study	Black Enrollment	Percent	Hispanic American Enrollment	Percent	Native American Enrollment	Percent	Asian American Enrollment	Percent	Total Enrollment
Arts and humanities	1,516	2.8	794	1.5	164	0.3	484	0.9	53,920
Education	6,990	7.2	1,113	1.2	384	0.4	587	0.6	96,568
Engineering	368	1.2	263	0.8	37	0.1	1,020	3.3	31,273
Health professions	727	5.5	164	1.2	76	0.6	260	2.0	13,238
Life sciences	419	1.5	247	0.9	62	0.2	519	1.9	27,641
Biology	(130)	(2.6)	(34)	(0.7)	(4)	(0.1)	(84)	(1.7)	(5,027)
Biochemistry	(22)	(1.2)	(11)	(0.6)	(5)	(0.3)	(57)	(3.2)	(1,804)
Microbiology	(33)	(1.8)	(17)	(0.9)	(6)	(0.3)	(57)	(3.2)	(1,801)
Physiology	(17)	(1.5)	(10)	(0.9)	(3)	(0.3)	(22)	(2.0)	(1,110)
Other	(191)	(1.2)	(145)	(0.9)	(34)	(0.2)	(253)	(1.6)	(15,504)
Mathematical sciences	305	2.5	78	0.6	23	0.2	262	2.1	12,446
Physical sciences	299	1.4	140	0.7	49	0.2	565	2.6	21,629
Chemistry	(129)	(1.6)	(53)	(0.7)	(15)	(0.2)	(253)	(3.2)	(8,040)
Physics	(68)	(1.2)	(31)	(0.6)	(12)	(0.2)	(169)	(3.0)	(5,559)
Other	(78)	(1.2)	(44)	(0.7)	(10)	(0.2)	(98)	(1.5)	(6,56ᴜ)
Basic social sciences	1,471	4.1	426	1.2	110	0.3	380	1.1	35,583
Economics	(109)	(1.9)	(47)	(0.8)	(15)	(0.3)	(92)	(1.6)	(5,766)
Psychology	(435)	(4.2)	(121)	(1.2)	(30)	(0.3)	(87)	(0.8)	(10,318)
Sociology	(263)	(5.8)	(89)	(2.0)	(10)	(0.2)	(61)	(1.3)	(4,566)
Other basic social sciences	(592)	(4.6)	(163)	(1.3)	(49)	(0.4)	(130)	(1.0)	(12,969)
All other fields	4,146	5.1	769	1.0	276	0.3	999	1.2	80,666
TOTAL, ALL FIELDS	16,241	4.4	3,994	1.1	1,181	0.3	1,181	1.4	372,964

Note: Based on data from 154 institutions able to provide minority enrollment data within field of study.

Figures in parentheses sum to less than their respective subtotals because some institutions could report data only for the total field category but not for subfields.

Source: Elaine H. El-Khawas and Joan L. Kinzer, Enrollment of Minority Graduate Students at Ph.D. Granting Institutions, (Washington, D.C.: American Council on Education, August 1974).

TABLE 6.18

Number Receiving Doctoral Degrees in 1973, by Citizenship and
Racial/Ethnic Identification

Citizenship	White/ Caucasian	Black[a]	Asian[b]	Latin[c]	Native American	All Other	Minority Total	Grand Total
U.S. citizens	26,400	760	320	228	148	12	1,468	27,868
Percent	94.7	2.7	1.15	0.8	.53	--	5.3	100.0
Non-U.S. citizens, immigration visas	826	56	1,067	23	0	12	1,158	1,984
Non-U.S. citizens, other visas	1,817	160	1,042	96	1	46	1,345	3,162
Total (citizenship and ethnicity known)	29,043	976	2,429	347	149	70	3,971	33,014
Citizenship and ethnicity unknown	--	--	--	--	--	--	--	713
TOTAL	29,043	976	2,429	347	149	70	3,971	33,727

Note: Data adjusted for partial response.
[a]Includes 12 individuals who indicated white, Indian, or other mixtures.
[b]Includes South Asians, to the extent these people so identified themselves.
[c]Includes Puerto Ricans, Spanish Americans, and Mexican Americans.
Source: Elaine H. El-Khawas and Joan L. Kinzer, "Enrollment of Minority Graduate Students at Ph.D. Granting Institutions" (Washington, D.C.: American Council on Education, August 1974).

TABLE 6.19

Doctorates Awarded in Historically Black Colleges, 1971-73

	1970-71	1971-72	1972-73
Zoology, general biology	7	9	11
Pharmacology	2	7	1
Physiology	3	--	2
Chemistry	8	5	9
Physics	4	4	2
Theology	2	--	4
English	5	1	1
African studies	2	1	2
Political science	3	--	4
History	2	--	3
Psychology	--	--	2
Counseling and guidance	1	1	2
Dental specialties (not D.D.S.)	8	--	--
Total doctorate degrees	47	28	43

Source: Elias Blake, Jr., et al., Degrees Granted and Enrollment Trends in Historically Black Colleges: An Eight Year Study, Vol. 1, no. 1 (Washington, D.C.: Institute for Service to Education, October 1974), p. 48.

TABLE 6.20

Professional Degrees Awarded in Historically Black Colleges
in Selected Fields, 1971-73

	1970-71	1971-72	1972-73
Law	164	195	259
Theology	59	47	67
Dentistry (D.D.S. or D.M.D.)	95	106	128
Medicine (M.D.)	160	176	173
Veterinary medicine (D.V.M.)	25	27	16
Total professional degrees	503	551	643

Source: Elias Blake, Jr., et al., Degrees Granted and Enrollment Trends in Historically Black Colleges: An Eight Year Study, Vol. 1, no. 1 (Washington, D.C.: Institute for Service to Education, October 1974), p. 48.

In terms of earned doctoral degrees received by the various ethnic groups in 1973, 760 or 2.7 percent were black; 320 or 1.15 percent were Asian American; 228 or 0.8 percent were Hispanic American, 148 or 0.53 percent were Native American; while 12 doctoral degrees were received by other minorities (see Table 6.18). The figures include doctorates received by U.S. citizens only. This point is very important because in reviews of the National Academy of Science's study of doctorates received in 1973, we find that Asians received 2,429 doctorates; however, only 320 of those were received by Asians who are U.S. citizens. We feel that given the number and percentage of Asian Americans who are enrolled in graduate school and who have completed their undergraduate education, the number and percentage of Asian Americans receiving the doctorate is very low.

ETHNIC GRADUATE SCHOOLS AND PROGRAMS

In 1974, 521 Native American students were sponsored by the Bureau of Indian Affairs, and in that same year 226 students earned graduate degrees. While the 1974 graduate enrollment sponsored by the BIA was only a 6.5 percent increase over the previous year, the number of students receiving graduate degrees increased 34.5 percent during that one year.

The historically black colleges in 1973 awarded 43 doctorates: 14 in the biological sciences, 11 in the physical sciences, 4 in theology, and 12 in the social sciences (see Table 6.19). It might be of interest to note that two doctorates were awarded in African studies and only two in education, despite the rather high percentage of blacks in education. A doctoral program in education would seem like a logical one for the black colleges; however, many education majors view the master's degree in education as a terminal degree. In 1973 the black colleges also awarded several first-time professional degrees: 259 in law, 67 in theology, 128 in dentistry, 173 in medicine, 16 veterinary medicine, for a total of 643 degrees (see Table 6.20). On the other hand, it is important to note that not all of these degrees were awarded to black or minority students, because there is a sizable number of white students enrolled in the professional schools at the historically black colleges.

7

HIGHER EDUCATION ENROLLMENT IN SELECTED STATES

For an in-depth study of states, California, Florida, Illinois, New York, and Texas were selected because of their size and representation of a variety of minority groups. California has a large population of blacks, Native Americans, Asian Americans, and Hispanic Americans; Florida has a large population of blacks, Cubans, and a small population of Native Americans and other Hispanic Americans; Illinois has a large black population and sizable Hispanic American and Native American populations; New York State has large black, Puerto Rican, and Asian American populations; while Texas has sizable black and Chicano populations.

The minority college enrollment in these five states is reviewed as well as one large metropolitan area within each state; and in a special case the minority enrollment in New York City is reviewed.

CALIFORNIA

In California we find that the largest minority group is Hispanic Americans, 15.5 percent of the total population, followed by blacks who constitute 7.0 percent, Asian Americans 2.7 percent, and Native Americans 0.4 percent (see Table 7.1). (SMSA data are available only for the year 1970 and only for blacks, Native Americans, and Asian Americans.)

In California as a whole there is a pattern of minority underrepresentation in college: blacks represent 7.0 percent of the population but comprise only 5.7 percent of the undergraduate enrollment; Asian Americans are 2.7 percent of the population and 4.7 percent of the undergraduate enrollment; Hispanic Americans comprise

TABLE 7.1

College Enrollment for California and the Los Angeles SMSA, 1970

Source	State/SMSA	White	Black	Hispanic American	Native American	Asian American	Total
			Population				
Census	State	14,834,573	1,398,498	3,101,589	88,271	534,784	19,957,715
	Percent	74.3	7.0	15.5	0.4	2.7	100.0
	Los Angeles	NA^a	762,844	NA	24,509	178,335	7,032,075
	Percent	--	10.8	--	0.3	2.5	100.0
			Undergraduate Enrollment^b				
Census	State	636,543	42,882	79,742	2,671	44,449	759,007
	Percent	83.8	5.6	10.5	0.4	5.9	100.0
	Los Angeles	207,709	22,446	32,762	719	15,850	262,917
	Percent	79.0	8.5	12.2	0.3	6.0	100.0
OCR	State	463,162	32,317	35,065	5,405	26,304	562,210
	Percent	82.4	5.7	6.2	1.0	4.7	100.0
			Graduate Enrollment				
Census	State	121,870	3,873	9,635	NA	NA	133,917
	Percent	90.0	2.9	7.2	--	--	100.0
	Los Angeles	NA	1,871	3,804	NA	NA	43,568
	Percent	--	4.1	8.4	--	--	100.0
OCR	State	49,156	1,695	1,442	286	2,067	54,646
	Percent	90.0	3.1	2.6	0.5	3.8	100.0

^aNA = not available.

^bCensus data on Native Americans and Asian Americans for the state and SMSA include both undergraduates and graduates; subtotals will not equal totals.

Sources: U.S. Bureau of the Census, "Detail Characteristics of the Population," U.S. and California, 1970, and "Special Subject Reports"; U.S. Department of Health, Education and Welfare, Office for Civil Rights, "Racial and Ethnic Enrollment Data from Institutions of Higher Education, Fall 1970," 1972.

15.5 percent of the population but only 6.2 percent of the undergraduate enrollment; Native Americans comprise 0.4 percent of
the population but 1.0 percent of the undergraduate enrollment. We
find in California, as with the nation as a whole, that the two most
severely underrepresented groups in college are the same: blacks
and Hispanic Americans. While the Asian American enrollment is
slightly higher than its representation in the total California population, we feel that Asians are underrepresented, given the large percentage of Asians who graduate from high schools and are in the top
half of their graduating classes. On the other hand, data regarding
Native Americans is not available or clear enough to make a competent assessment about representation. We believe there has been a
critical undercounting of Native Americans in California and that
the percentage of Indians in California should be much greater than
the 0.7 percent indicated by the 1970 Census.

At the graduate level the minority groups are still underrepresented. Native Americans have a 0.3 percent enrollment at the
graduate level, blacks 3.6 percent, Asian Americans 2.1 percent,
and Hispanic Americans 3.7 percent. While these data indicate
across-the-board underrepresentation within the California graduate
schools for all minorities, we find data on Asian Americans a little
disturbing. First, the percentage of Asian students who enroll in
graduate school is lower than its percentage in the state, 2.1 in
graduate school versus 2.7 in the state. This concern is based on
the fact that at the undergraduate level Asian American enrollment
is well over their representation in the state.

Data on graduate enrollment within the Los Angeles metropolitan area in 1970 indicated that 4.1 percent of all graduate students
were black and 8.4 percent were Hispanic American. This trend as
in the state indicated underrepresented enrollment of these two
groups in Los Angeles metropolitan area graduate schools.

FLORIDA

In Florida we found that 15.3 percent of the population was
black, 0.2 percent Asian American, 6.6 percent Hispanic American, and 0.1 percent Native American (see Table 7.2). Blacks and
Hispanic Americans are underrepresented in institutions of higher
education. There is one bit of information about the black college
undergraduate enrollment data in Florida that should be explained:
At the university level blacks are overrepresented, because the
black college, Florida Agricultural and Mechanical University, is
classified as a university rather than a four-year college. The college enrollments for Native Americans, 251, and Asian Americans,

TABLE 7.2

College Enrollment for Florida and the Miami SMSA, 1970

Source	State/SMSA	White	Black	Hispanic American	Native American	Asian American	Total
				Population			
Census	State	5,277,237	1,041,966	451,382	6,196	12,631	6,789,412
	Percent	77.7	15.3	6.6	0.1	0.2	100.0
	Miami	NA[a]	189,666	NA	1,085	2,757	1,267,792
	Percent	--	5.0	--	0.1	0.2	100.0
				Undergraduate Enrollment[b]			
Census	State	143,104	15,521	11,677	NA	NA	170,302
	Percent	84.0	9.1	6.7	--	--	100.0
	Miami	135,758	8,790	31,240	--	--	175,788
	Percent	77.2	5.0	17.8	--	--	100.0
OCR	State	118,796	12,740	4,820	251	599	137,206
	Percent	86.6	9.3	3.5	0.2	0.4	100.0
				Graduate Enrollment			
Census	State	17,792	868	1,316	NA	NA	18,945
	Percent	93.9	4.6	6.9	--	--	100.0
	Miami	NA	146	496	NA	NA	3,630
	Percent	--	4.0	13.7	--	--	100.0
OCR	State	5,470	202	207	14	191	6,084
	Percent	89.9	3.3	3.4	0.2	3.3	100.0

[a]NA = not available.

[b]Data taken from separate tables, therefore subtotals will not equal totals.

Sources: U.S. Bureau of the Census, "Detail Characteristics of the Population," U.S. and Florida, 1970, and "Special Subject Reports"; U.S. Department of Health, Education and Welfare, Office for Civil Rights, "Racial and Ethnic Enrollment Data from Institutions of Higher Education, Fall 1970," 1972.

599, are considered too small to make valid judgments about their distribution in Florida institutions of higher education. In the Miami metropolitan area blacks and Hispanic Americans are also under-represented in institutions of higher education.

At the graduate level in Florida there were 14 Native Americans enrolled in graduate schools, 202 blacks, 191 Asian Americans, and 207 Hispanic Americans. In the Miami area the 1970 Census data indicated a 5.0 percent black graduate enrollment, a 0.1 percent Native American enrollment, and a 0.2 percent Asian American enrollment.

ILLINOIS

In Illinois the major minority groups are blacks and Hispanic Americans: 1,422,353 blacks for 12.8 percent, 364,397 Hispanic Americans for 3.3 percent, 9,756 Native Americans for 0.1 percent, and 47,486 Asian Americans for 0.4 percent (see Table 7.3). In the Chicago metropolitan area the 1970 Census listed 1,230,919 blacks, 8,996 Native Americans, and 39,768 Asian Americans. The 1970 Census did not record a racial count for Hispanic Americans in the Chicago metropolitan area.

At the undergraduate level in the state of Illinois the Office for Civil Rights' 1970 survey of undergraduate student enrollment reveals that there were 1,213 Native Americans for 0.5 percent and 2,069 Hispanic American undergraduates for 0.8 percent, while the 1970 Census Bureau undergraduate survey listed 28,094 blacks for 8.5 percent and 5,727 Hispanic American undergraduates for 1.7 percent.

In the Chicago metropolitan area there were 23,293 black college students and 4,556 Hispanic American undergraduates. No figures were available on the undergraduate enrollments of Native American and Asian students.

According to the Office for Civil Rights, at the graduate level in Illinois for the year 1970 there were 53 Native Americans enrolled in graduate schools for 0.2 percent, 1,240 blacks for 5.1 percent, 468 Asian Americans for 1.9 percent, and 205 Hispanic Americans for 0.8 percent. These figures were reported by the Office for Civil Rights' survey of graduate student enrollment. Also in 1970 the Census Bureau reported that there were 2,267 black graduate students for 4.1 percent and 1,130 Hispanic Americans for 2.2 percent of the graduate student population. The Census Bureau also reported that for the Chicago metropolitan area there were 1,740 black graduate students for 4.8 percent and 850 Hispanic American graduate students for 2.4 percent. These data for Illinois

TABLE 7.3

College Enrollment for Illinois and the Chicago SMSA, 1970

Source	State/SMSA	White	Black	Hispanic American	Native American	Asian American	Total
		Population					
Census	State	9,265,943	1,422,353	364,397	9,756	47,486	11,109,935
	Percent	83.4	12.8	3.3	0.1	0.4	100.0
	Chicago	NA[a]	1,230,919	NA	8,996	39,768	6,978,947
	Percent	--	17.6	--	0.1	0.6	100.0
		Undergraduate Enrollment[b]					
Census	State	297,529	28,094	5,727	290	3,825	331,350
	Percent	89.8	8.5	1.7	0.1	1.2	100.0
	Chicago	152,089	23,293	4,556	209	2,744	179,938
	Percent	84.5	12.9	2.5	0.1	1.5	100.0
OCR	State	219,173	21,420	2,069	1,213	1,995	245,870
	Percent	89.1	8.7	0.8	0.5	0.8	100.0
		Graduate Enrollment					
Census	State	50,944	2,267	1,130	NA	NA	54,954
	Percent	92.7	4.1	2.2	--	--	100.0
	Chicago	NA	1,740	853	NA	NA	36,022
	Percent	--	4.8	2.4	--	--	100.0
OCR	State	22,545	1,240	205	53	468	24,511
	Percent	92.0	5.1	0.8	0.2	1.9	100.0

[a]NA = not available.
[b]Census data on Native Americans and Asian Americans for the state and SMSA include both undergraduates and graduates; subtotals will not equal totals.

Sources: U.S. Bureau of the Census, "Detail Characteristics of the Population," U.S. and Illinois, 1970, and "Special Subject Reports"; U.S. Department of Health, Education and Welfare, Office for Civil Rights, "Racial and Ethnic Enrollment Data from Institutions of Higher Education, Fall 1970," 1972.

at both the graduate and undergraduate levels follow enrollment
trends at the national level which show underrepresentation of
minority-group individuals.

NEW YORK

In New York State for the year 1970 there were 2,164,560
blacks for 11.9 percent of the total population, 872,471 Hispanic
Americans for 4.9 percent, 25,266 Native Americans for 0.1 percent, and 122,652 Asian Americans for 0.7 percent (see Table 7.4).
In the New York City metropolitan area (SMSA) there were 1,885,303
blacks for 16.3 percent of the metropolitan population, 12,160 Native
Americans for 0.1 percent, and 105,901 Asian Americans for 0.9
percent. In New York City (1970) there were 1,664,574 blacks for
21 percent and 811,843 Hispanic Americans for 10.2 percent of the
New York City population.

In reviewing college enrollment in New York State we will de-
viate from our normal pattern and will consider the enrollment in
New York City and outside of the city. This mode of analysis is
based on the fact that in New York State there are two state-operated
higher education systems.

In 1970 the Office for Civil Rights' survey of higher education
revealed that New York State minority undergraduate enrollments
were 0.3 percent Native American, 5.8 percent black, 1.1 percent
Asian American, and 2.2 percent Hispanic American. During that
same year the Census Bureau indicated that for New York State there
were 36,270 black undergraduate students comprising 6.6 percent of
the state's undergraduate enrollment and 8,591 Hispanic Americans
for 1.6 percent. In the New York City metropolitan area the Census
reported that 8.6 percent undergraduates were black (14,618) and
2.0 percent were Spanish (3,460).

New York State's undergraduate enrollments are separated into
two categories: namely, those enrolled in the State University of
New York system (SUNY) and those enrolled in the City University
of New York's system (CUNY) (Stent and Brown 1974). At the undergraduate level 0.2 percent of SUNY students were Native American as was 0.2 percent of CUNY's enrollment. Of SUNY's enrollment 3.6 percent were black; 13.8 percent of CUNY's were.
SUNY was 0.3 percent Asian American; CUNY 2.6 percent,
while of SUNY's enrollment 0.9 percent were Hispanic American, versus 5.5 percent at CUNY. It is clear that the City University of New York has the largest minority undergraduate enrollment of the two systems in the state. In 1972, 64 percent
of the CUNY undergraduate students were white, 22.4 percent

TABLE 7.4

College Enrollment for New York and the New York City SMSA, 1970

Source	State/SMSA	White	Black	Hispanic American	Native American	Asian American	Total
		Population					
Census	State	15,052,002	2,164,560	872,471	25,266	122,652	18,236,951
	Percent	82.5	11.9	4.9	0.1	0.7	100.0
	New York City SMSA	NAa	1,885,303	NA	12,160	105,901	11,571,899
	Percent	—	16.3	—	0.1	0.9	100.0
	New York City	NA	1,664,574	811,843	NA	NA	7,894,798
	Percent	—	21.0	10.2	—	—	100.0
		Undergraduate Enrollmentb					
Census	State	507,851	36,270	8,591	683	8,903	552,712
	Percent	91.9	6.6	1.6	0.1	1.6	100.0
	New York City SMSA	150,054	14,618	3,460	343	7,250	169,137
	Percent	88.7	8.6	2.0	0.2	0.4	100.0
OCR	State	384,055	24,758	9,231	1,221	4,516	423,781
	Percent	90.6	5.8	2.2	0.3	1.1	100.0
		Graduate Enrollment					
Census	State	100,239	3,434	506	NA	NA	106,577
	Percent	94.5	3.2	0.5	—	—	100.0
	New York City SMSA	NA	2,897	448	NA	NA	72,538
	Percent	—	3.9	0.6	—	—	100.0
OCR	State	8,061	1,443	493	145	886	8,454
	Percent	95.4	3.7	1.3	0.4	2.2	100.0

aNA = not available.
bCensus data on Native Americans and Asian Americans for the state and SMSA include both undergraduates and graduates; subtotals will not equal totals.

Sources: U.S. Bureau of the Census, "Detail Characteristics of the Population," U.S. and New York, 1970, and "Special Subject Reports"; U.S. Department of Health, Education and Welfare, Office for Civil Rights, "Racial and Ethnic Enrollment Data from Institutions of Higher Education, Fall 1970," 1972.

were black, 6.9 percent were Puerto Ricans, 1.8 percent were other
Hispanic Americans, 0.3 percent were Native Americans, and 2.4
percent were Asian Americans.

On the graduate level in 1970, New York State enrolled 145
Native Americans which constituted 0.4 percent of the total graduate
student population, 1,433 blacks for 3.7 percent, 886 Asian Americans for 2.2 percent, and 493 Hispanic Americans for 1.3 percent.
Those were figures published by the Office for Civil Rights; however,
the Census Bureau reported that 3,434 blacks were enrolled in
graduate schools in New York State for 3.2 percent of the graduate
population and 506 Hispanic Americans for 0.5 percent. In that same
year Census data revealed that in the New York City metropolitan
area (SMSA) there were 2,897 black graduate students for 3.9 percent and 448 Hispanic Americans for 0.6 percent. These data speak
for themselves in that minorities are underrepresented at both the
graduate and undergraduate level in New York State.

TEXAS

In 1970 the general population in Texas was 68.8 percent white,
12.5 percent black, 18.4 percent Hispanic American, 0.2 percent
Native American, and 0.1 percent Asian American (see Table 7.5).
In the Houston metropolitan area the population was 19.3 percent
black, 0.2 percent Native American, and 0.3 percent Asian American.
Separate data on the Spanish surnamed in Houston were not available.

The undergraduate enrollment in Texas for 1970 collected by
the Office for Civil Rights' survey was 0.7 percent Native American,
7.8 percent black, 0.5 percent Asian American, and 7.8 percent
Hispanic American. In that same year the Census Bureau reported
that the undergraduate enrollment for the state was 81.4 percent
white, 7.8 percent black, and 10.6 percent Hispanic American. In
the Houston metropolitan area the undergraduate enrollment was
85.8 percent white, 9.2 percent black, and 5.0 percent Hispanic
American.

The graduate enrollment for Texas in 1970 reported by the Office for Civil Rights was 0.4 percent Native American, 3.1 percent
black, 1.6 percent Asian American, 3.7 percent Hispanic American.
The Census Bureau in 1970 reported that the graduate enrollment was
93.9 percent white, 3.8 percent black, and 7.6 percent Hispanic
American. In the Houston metropolitan area the 1970 Census reported that the graduate enrollment for minorities was 8.3 percent
black and 5.4 percent Hispanic American. Ethnic graduate enrollment data for other minority groups were not given.

TABLE 7.5

College Enrollment for Texas and the Houston SMSA, 1970

Source	State/SMSA	White	Black	Hispanic American	Native American	Asian American	Total
		Population					
Census	State	7,707,518	1,396,605	2,059,671	17,031	14,606	11,195,431
	Percent	68.8	12.5	18.4	0.2	0.1	100.0
	Houston	NA[a]	382,382	NA	3,215	5,638	1,958,031
	Percent	--	19.3	--	0.2	0.3	100.0
		Undergraduate Enrollment[b]					
Census	State	252,358	24,160	33,318	340	NA	309,836
	Percent	81.4	7.8	10.6	0.1	--	100.0
	Houston	234,646	25,051	13,797	50	NA	273,494
	Percent	85.8	9.2	5.0	--	--	100.0
OCR	State	236,558	22,282	22,054	1,851	NA	284,189
	Percent	88.1	7.8	7.8	0.7	--	100.0
		Graduate Enrollment					
Census	State	38,391	1,560	3,110	NA	NA	40,832
	Percent	93.9	3.8	7.6	--	--	100.0
	Houston	NA	643	461	NA	NA	7,714
	Percent	--	8.3	5.4	--	--	100.0
OCR	State	13,178	444	534	61	230	14,447
	Percent	91.2	3.1	3.7	0.4	1.6	100.0

[a]NA = not available.

[b]Census data on Native Americans and Asian Americans for the state and SMSA include both undergraduates and graduates; subtotals will not equal totals.

Sources: U.S. Bureau of the Census, "Detail Characteristics of the Population," U.S. and Texas, 1970, and "Special Subject Reports"; U.S. Department of Health, Education and Welfare, Office for Civil Rights, "Racial and Ethnic Enrollment Data from Institutions of Hither Education, Fall 1970," 1972.

Data on undergraduate and graduate enrollment in Texas reveal that minorities are severely underrepresented in institutions of higher education. Texas is unique from the other states with the exception of Florida in that there are several large black colleges still operating. Many undergraduate and graduate students in Texas may be found at Texas Southern and Prairie View universities and several other black four-year and two-year colleges. On the other hand, these data for Texas and Florida reveal that there was minority underrepresentation in institutions of higher education regardless of the state black colleges.

SUMMARY

Our review of California, Florida, Illinois, New York, and Texas reveals some interesting phenomena. In two of the states, California and New York (New York City only), public education was largely tuition-free. Yet, we still find significant minority underrepresentation in institutions of higher education in California and New York State. On the other hand, in Florida and Texas we find significant numbers of blacks attending black colleges, but still we find significant black underrepresentation in institutions of higher education in those two states. This information suggests that despite the schooling arrangement for higher education--black or nonblack colleges--or the funding arrangement for higher education--tuition-free and tuition charges--minorities still find it difficult to enter these institutions in representative numbers. A look at enrollment trends in the five states between 1968 and 1970 reveals that in California the Native American undergraduate student enrollment increased 82.9 percent, the black undergraduate enrollment declined 0.5 percent, the Asian American enrollment increased 24 percent, and the Hispanic American undergraduate population increased 11 percent. In Florida the undergraduate enrollment between 1968 and 1970 showed that the Native American undergraduate student population declined 71.1 percent, the black undergraduate enrollment increased 14.5 percent, the Asian American enrollment increased 71.9 percent, and the Hispanic American enrollment declined 29.6 percent for that two-year period. In Illinois for that same two-year period the minority enrollment showed an increase of 34.8 percent for Native Americans, a 36.2 percent increase for blacks, a 9.6 percent increase for Asian Americans, and a 25.8 percent increase for Hispanic Americans. In New York State for that same two-year period the percent change in enrollment was 34.9 percent increase for Native Americans, 90 percent increase for blacks, 51.1 percent increase for Asian Americans, and 75.1 percent increase for Hispanic

TABLE 7.6

Native American Undergraduate Enrollment from Two
Data Sources: U.S. Census and OCR, 1970

Location	Enrollment	Percent Enrollment	Percent 18-24 Year- Old Group Enrollment
United States (763,594/0.4)			
Census	14,191	0.23	14.8
OCR	27,263	0.45	28.4
California (88,263/0.4)			
Census	2,671	0.40	20.1
OCR	5,405	1.00	40.7
Illinois (10,304/0.1)			
Census	280	0.10	19.0
OCR	1,213	0.50	79.3
New York (25,560/0.1)			
Census	683	0.10	22.6
OCR	1,221	0.30	40.4
Texas (16,921)			
Census	340	0.10	13.1
Florida			
OCR	251	0.20	--

Note: Figures in parentheses represent the Native American
population, number/percent of total.
Source: U.S. Bureau of the Census, School Enrollment, 1970;
U.S. Department of Health, Education and Welfare, Office for Civil
Rights, "Racial and Ethnic Enrollment Data from Institutions of
Higher Education, Fall 1970," 1972; and U.S. Bureau of the Census,
Subject Reports, American Indians in the U.S., PC (2)-1F, June 1973.

Americans. It appears that in New York the enrollment of substantial
numbers of minorities in institutions of higher education is a relatively new phenomenon. In Texas for the two-year period the percent
change in enrollment was a decline of 45.5 percent for Native Americans, an increase of 1.7 percent for blacks, a decline of 15.8 percent
for Asian Americans, and an increase of 2.7 percent for Hispanic
Americans. Overall for Texas there was a decline of 1.7 percent in
total minority enrollment during that two-year period. However, data
on Native Americans from several sources were inconsistent (see
Table 7.6).

8

**ECONOMIC
INDICATORS AND
THE MINORITY
COLLEGE STUDENT**

ECONOMIC INDICATORS

A look at major economic indicators such as earned income,
unemployment rate, and underemployment rate that affect members
of the minority community shows that economically minorities are
not doing well in the United States. In general, minorities earn only
a fraction of the income earned by white Americans (see Table 8.1);
their unemployment rate is more than twice that for white individuals
(see Table 8.2); and for those who are employed they are likely to be
working less hours and earning less money than their white counterparts. Many minority individuals have been unemployed so long that
they are no longer counted among the employable or the unemployed
(they have become invisible people). While the data on Asian Americans may appear to put them in a favored position economically,
they are not; for example, the 1970 Census listed the median family
income for Japanese Americans as $12,515, for Chinese Americans
$10,615, for Filipino Americans $9,318, and for white Americans
$9,596. These data seem to put the Asian Americans in favorable
light compared to white Americans, but when one considers the fact
that Asian Americans on the average have a much higher educational
level than the general white population, we have to conclude that they
have not achieved economically what they should be achieving.
Further, a study by the U.S. Civil Rights Commission (Sillas 1975)
among Asian people on the West Coast indicated that many college-
trained Asian Americans, especially Filipino Americans, who im-
migrate to this country find that they cannot find suitable occupations
upon arrival in the United States. For example, many Asian people
who were doctors, lawyers, and dentists in their native homeland
have to settle for menial and sometimes domestic work in the United
States.

TABLE 8.1

Median Income of Families, 1964-74
(in current dollars)

| Year | Race of Head of Household | | | Ratio of Black and Other Races to White | Ratio of Black to White |
	Black and Other Races	Black	White		
1964	3,839	3,724	6,858	0.56	0.54
1965	3,994	3,886	7,251	0.55	0.54
1966	4,674	4,507	7,792	0.60	0.58
1967	5,094	4,875	8,234	0.62	0.59
1968	5,590	5,360	8,937	0.63	0.60
1969	6,191	5,999	9,794	0.63	0.61
1970	6,516	6,279	10,236	0.64	0.61
1971	6,714	6,440	10,672	0.63	0.60
1972	7,106	6,864	11,549	0.62	0.59
1973	7,596	7,269	12,595	0.60	0.58
1974	8,265	7,808	13,356	0.62	0.58

Source: U.S. Bureau of the Census, Current Population Reports, "The Social and Economic Status of the Black Population in the United States, 1974," Special Studies, Series P-23, No. 54 (Washington, D.C.: U.S. Government Printing Office, 1975), p. 25.

TABLE 8.2

Unemployment Rates, by Sex and Age, 1973 and 1974
(annual averages)

Sex, Age, and Race	1973	1974
Black and other races	8.9	9.9
Men, 20 years and over	5.7	6.8
Women, 20 years and over	8.2	8.4
Both sexes, 16 to 19 years	30.2	32.9
Black	9.3	10.4
Men, 20 years and over	5.9	7.3
Women, 20 years and over	8.5	8.7
Both sexes, 16 to 19 years	31.4	34.9
White	4.3	5.0
Men, 20 years and over	2.9	3.5
Women, 20 years and over	4.3	5.0
Both sexes, 16 to 19 years	12.6	14.0
Ratio of black and other races to white	2.2	2.1
Men, 20 years and over	2.0	2.1
Women, 20 years and over	2.0	1.7
Both sexes 16 to 19 years	2.5	2.5

Source: U.S. Bureau of the Census, Current Population Reports, "The Social and Economic Status of the Black Population in the United States, 1974," Special Studies, Series P-23, No. 54 (Washington, D.C.: U.S. Government Printing Office, 1975), Table 39.

TABLE 8.3

Family Members 18 to 24 Years Old, by College Enrollment Status
and Family Income, 1974

(percentages)

Enrollment Status and Race	Under $5,000	Family Income in 1973			Total Reporting on Family Income
		$5,000 to $9,999	$10,000 to $14,999	$15,000 and Over	
Black total, 18 to 24 years					
(in thousands)	668	525	270	193	1,653
Enrolled in college	17	30	26	42	25
Not enrolled in college	83	70	74	58	75
High school graduate	37	49	56	50	46
Not high school graduate	46	21	18	8	29
White total, 18 to 24 years					
(in thousands)	855	1,702	2,422	4,388	9,320
Enrolled in college	17	27	37	50	39
Not enrolled in college	83	73	63	50	61
High school graduate	44	53	52	45	48
Not high school graduate	39	21	11	5	13

Source: U.S. Bureau of the Census, Current Population Reports, "The Social and Economic Status of the Black Population in the United States, 1974," Special Studies, Series P-23, No. 54 (Washington, D.C.: U.S. Government Printing Office, 1975), Table 66.

TABLE 8.4

Persons in the United States Below the Low-Income Level, 1969-74
(persons as of the following year)

Year	Number (thousands)			Percent Below the Low-Income Level		
	Black and Other Races	Black	White	Black and Other Races	Black	White
1969	7,488	7,467	16,659	31.0	32.2	9.5
1970	7,936	7,548	17,484	32.0	33.5	9.9
1971	7,780	7,396	17,780	30.9	32.5	9.9
1972	8,257	7,710	16,203	31.9	33.3	9.0
1973	7,831	7,388	15,142	29.6	31.4	8.4
1974	7,970	7,467	16,290	29.5	31.4	8.9

Note: The low-income threshold for a nonfarm family of four was $5,038 in 1974, $4,540 in 1973, and $2,973 in 1959. Families and unrelated individuals are classified as being above or below the low-income threshold, using the poverty index adopted by a Federal Interagency Committee in 1969. This index centers around the Department of Agriculture's Economy Food Plan and reflects the differing consumption requirements of families based on their composition, sex, and age of the family head, and farm-nonfarm residence. The low-income cutoffs for farm families have been set at 85 percent of the nonfarm levels. These cutoffs are up-dated every year to reflect the changes in the Consumer Price Index. The low-income data excluded inmates of institutions, members of the armed forces living in barracks, and unrelated individuals under 14 years of age.

Source: U.S. Bureau of the Census, Current Population Reports, "The Social and Economic Status of the Black Population in the United States, 1974," Special Studies, Series P-23, No. 54 (Washington, D.C.: U.S. Government Printing Office, 1975), Table 23.

TABLE 8.5

Income in 1974 of All Families and Families with Head of
Spanish Origin, United States
(percentages)

Family Income	Families with Head of Spanish Origin				Total Families
	Total	Mexican Origin	Puerto Rican Origin	Other Spanish Origin*	
Total families (thousands)	2,477	1,429	405	644	55,712
Percent:					
Less than $4,000	14.9	15.0	18.5	12.3	9.0
$4,000 to $6,999	19.4	19.2	26.4	15.2	13.0
$7,000 to $9,999	18.4	18.8	21.2	16.0	13.9
$10,000 to $14,999	24.3	26.6	18.0	23.0	24.4
$15,000 or more	23.1	20.4	15.8	33.5	39.7
Median income	$9,559	$9,498	$7,629	$11,410	$12,836

*Includes Cuban, Central or South American, and other Spanish origin.
Source: U.S. Bureau of the Census, Current Population Reports,
"Persons of Spanish Origin in the United States," Series P-20, No. 280
(Washington, D.C.: U.S. Government Printing Office, April 1975), Table 6.

TABLE 8.6

Persons by Type of Spanish Origin and Low-Income Status,
United States and Five Southwestern States, 1973
(numbers in thousands; persons as of March 1974)

	All Income Levels	Below Low-Income Level	Percent Below Low-Income Level
United States			
Mexican	6,455	1,516	23.5
Puerto Rican	1,548	528	34.1
Cuban	689	52	7.5
Central or South American	705	95	13.4
Other Spanish origin	1,398	175	12.5
Total, Spanish origin	10,785	2,366	21.9
Five Southwestern States			
Mexican	5,576	1,332	23.9
Total, Spanish origin	6,462	1,437	22.2

Source: U.S. Bureau of the Census, Current Population Reports,
"Characteristics of the Low-Income Population: 1973," Series P-60, No. 98
(Washington, D.C.: U.S. Government Printing Office, 1975), Table 47.

120

We find that data on major economic indicators among the major minority groups in this country are so commonplace that we do not feel the necessity to cite specific details on the subject at this time. We wish only to remind the reader that <u>in general</u> the minority groups in this country constitute an economically disadvantaged group (see Tables 8.3, 8.4, 8.5, and 8.6). We underline the comment in general, because minorities are not a monolithic group, there are differences between groups, and there are differences within groups. One could find minority individuals in these groups who are more like the general population and who may in many ways identify economically more with others than with their own ethnic group. We say this just to caution that all minorities are not alike, all minorities are not disadvantaged economically, nor are they educationally disadvantaged.

EDUCATIONAL COSTS

If the United States desires to upgrade the economic and educational opportunities for minority-group individuals it must provide the resources necessary to achieve that goal. We would like to make a special note that current economic indicators on Native Americans and Asian Americans are not available beyond the 1969 data collected by the Census Bureau. Therefore, we can present only the most current economic indicators on the black and Hispanic American populations. It should be noted that special studies by the U.S. Census are made available between the decennial surveys on the black and Hispanic American populations. We cannot expect another in-depth analysis of the economic conditions of Native Americans and Asians before the 1980 Census survey; and then the data will not be available until 1983, approximately three years after the survey has been completed. However, it is felt that inferences drawn from the 1970 data are still sufficiently sound for us to make our case regarding economic conditions among Native Americans and Asian Americans.

The ability to attend an institution of higher education in the United States requires considerable financial resources on the part of the individuals who wish to attend those institutions. Individuals who need the required admissions costs for the college or university of their choice are generally required to reimburse that institution for services rendered, namely, for instructional and other related costs. Therefore, the statement that all qualified individuals in the United States may attend college needs refinement and qualification. The statement should read, "The ability to attend college in the United States requires that an individual meet the

101832

admissions requirement of that institution and that such individual
have the resources available to reimburse the college for services
rendered."

What are the costs required to attend college and universities
in the United States? The Census Bureau in its 1973 Current Population Report listed the cost of attending institutions of higher education in the United States as $910 for attending a university, $1,318
to attend a four-year college, $410 to attend a two-year college, and
$533 to attend a vocational school (see Tables 8.7 and 8.8). These
figures include charges for tuition and fees, books and supplies, and
transportation only. They do not include living expenses such as
room and board or dormitory costs.

TABLE 8.7

Median Expected Educational Expenses by Type of College,
Attendance Status, and Control of School, October 1973
(dollars)

Median Educational Expenses	All Colleges	University	Four-Year College	Two-Year College
Public	721	825	859	401
Private	2,108	2,168	2,193	814
Total	834	912	1,323	410

Source: U.S. Bureau of the Census, Current Population Reports,
"Income and Expenses of Students Enrolled in Postsecondary Schools:
October, 1973," Series P-20, No. 281 (Washington, D.C.: U.S.
Government Printing Office, 1975), p. 4.

In the 1974–75 school year the American Council on Education
estimated that the mean costs including room and board were $1,220
to attend a public two-year college, $1,610 to attend a public four-
year college, $1,850 to attend a public university (see Table 8.9).
The total mean costs for attending private institutions of higher education were $2,880 to attend a two-year college, $3,400 to attend a
four-year college, and $4,060 to attend a university. These figures
clearly indicate that it is very expensive to attend college. First,
monies generated to pursue a college education can be generated only
from an individual's net income--monies from income sources after
taxes. However, for a large percentage of economically disadvantaged

TABLE 8.8

Educational Expenses for Postsecondary Students
by Type of School, October 1973
(dollars)

| Type of School | Total | Median Educational Expenses | | |
		Tuition and Fees	Books and Supplies	Transportation
University	910	650	141	100
Four-year college	1,318	989	142	101
Two-year college	410	169	89	114
Vocational school	533	317	58	76
Total	784	549	124	102

Source: U.S. Bureau of the Census, Current Population Reports, "Income and Expenses of Students Enrolled in Postsecondary Schools: October 1973," Series P-20, No. 281 (Washington, D.C.: U.S. Government Printing Office, 1975), Table E.

TABLE 8.9

Mean Educational Costs to Undergraduates, Public and Private
Institutions, by Selected Characteristics, 1974-75
(costs rounded to nearest ten dollars)

| Characteristics | Public | | Private | |
	Mean Undergraduate Tuition (in-state)	Mean Room and Board	Mean Undergraduate Tuition	Mean Room and Board
Type of institution				
Two-year	300	920	1,700	1,180
Four-year	550	1,060	2,170	1,230
University	620	1,230	2,620	1,440
Students receiving less than 20 percent need-based assistance	300	960	2,390	1,290
20-39	400	1,000	2,350	1,320
40-59	520	1,040	2,080	1,220
60-79	540	950	2,030	1,170
80-100	610	1,000	1,610	1,090
TOTAL	400	990	2,110	1,230

Source: American Council on Education, Student Assistance Participants and Programs 1974-75, Higher Education Panel Reports, December 1975.

minority individuals free tuition would still mean that many of those
individuals would not have the needed resources to attend college.

The ACE survey also revealed that to attend a public two-year
college the cost for room and board is $920, $1,060 to attend a four-
year college, and $1,230 to attend a public university. To attend
private institutions of higher education dormitory costs are $1,180
for a two-year college, $1,230 for a four-year college, and $1,440
for a private university. In addition to these costs students must
also have funds for miscellaneous items and general "spending
monies."

Currently, college students, at least those who qualify, may
apply for financial assistance from a variety of sources, which include: the federal government with a series of programs funded
through the U.S. Office of Education, state and local government
sources, and private foundations or donors. Generally speaking,
the major criteria for getting help to attend college are being economically disadvantaged and/or educationally disadvantaged. Fed-
erally financed assistance programs tend to utilize exclusively the
economic criterion, while local and state government assistance
programs tend to utilize both criteria.

The ACE survey of college assistance programs found that
38.8 percent of all assistance to college students comes from federal
sources, 26 percent from institutional sources, 6.8 percent from
tuition waivers, 19.7 percent from state and local government
sources, and 8.6 percent from private donors (see Table 8.10).
These data also reveal that from federal sources 68.5 percent of all
public two-year college students receive support from the federal
government compared to only 45.9 percent for those students who
attend public four-year colleges and 38.3 percent for all students
who attend public universities. In the private institutions, 50.7 percent of the two-year students receive help from the federal government compared to 30.8 percent who attend private four-year colleges and 27.2 percent who attend private universities. However,
financial aid from the colleges and universities themselves are given
mainly to students who attend four-year colleges and universities
(both public and private). Because the federal government uses the
economic disadvantageness criterion, it appears that a larger percentage of students enrolled in two-year institutions come from
economically disadvantaged families compared to those who are
enrolled in four-year colleges and universities.

If we view these data on the percentage of students receiving
aid under the federal government assistance programs, relative to
minority college students, we find that 33.6 percent of minorities
receive assistance from such programs compared to 66.4 percent
for the nonminority population (see Table 8.11). In view of the fact

TABLE 8.10

Source and Amount of Funds Available for Undergraduate and Graduate Students, by Type and Control of Institution, 1974–75
(percentages)

Source of Funds	Public Institutions				Private Institutions				Total Institutions
	Total	Two-Year	Four-Year	University	Total	Two-Year	Four-Year	University	
Total dollar amount (in millions)	2,026.7	349.8	850.5	826.4	1,900.1	78.8	1,223.7	597.6	3,926.8
Distribution									
Federal sources*	46.9	68.5	45.9	38.3	30.4	50.7	30.8	27.2	38.8
Institutional sources Direct	21.6	9.9	19.7	28.8	30.7	16.0	31.7	30.7	26.0
Tuition waivers and remissions	4.6	3.4	3.4	6.5	9.1	4.9	6.9	13.9	6.8
State and local government sources	18.7	13.2	22.2	17.3	20.7	23.5	21.6	18.5	19.7
Private donors	8.2	5.0	8.7	9.1	9.1	4.8	9.0	9.7	8.6

*Not included are programs which are not part of the revenue or expenditure accounts of institutions, for example, Veterans Educational Benefits, Social Security Student Benefits, Guaranteed Student Loans.

Source: American Council on Education, Student Assistance Participants and Programs 1974–75, Higher Education Panel Reports, No. 27, December 1975.

TABLE 8.11

Characteristics of All Students (Unduplicated Count) Receiving Aid under
Office of Education Assistance Programs, by Type and
Control of Institution, 1974–75
(percentages)

Characteristics	Public Institutions				Private Institutions				Total Institutions
	Total	Two-Year	Four-Year	University	Total	Two-Year	Four-Year	University	
Total	1,034,000	335,000	419,000	280,000	551,000	36,000	420,000	94,000	1,584,000
Ethnic group									
Minority	38.3	49.4	38.0	24.7	24.8	25.5	24.8	24.7	33.6
Nonminority	61.7	50.6	62.0	75.3	75.2	74.5	75.2	75.3	66.4
Sex									
Female	52.3	56.5	50.6	49.3	48.7	50.0	49.9	42.6	51.0
Male	47.7	43.5	49.4	50.7	51.3	50.0	50.1	57.4	49.0
Status									
Dependent under- graduates family income									
Less than $7,500	35.6	33.0	41.8	31.3	28.2	38.0	28.6	22.7	33.3
$7,500–$11,999	24.4	24.5	23.6	25.3	25.8	31.1	26.3	21.6	24.8
More than $11,999	14.0	12.9	13.6	16.5	30.0	21.0	32.2	24.4	19.1
Independent under- graduates	22.0	29.6	16.2	17.4	9.3	9.9	8.5	12.4	18.0
Graduate students	3.9	--	4.8	9.5	6.8	--	4.5	18.9	4.8

Note: "Unduplicated Count" excludes Guaranteed Student Loan program.
Source: American Council on Education, Student Assistance Participants and Programs 1974–75, Higher Education
Panel Reports, No. 27, December 1975.

that minorities constitute only 16 percent of the U.S. population, these figures clearly indicate that a disproportionate number of minority college students are from economically disadvantaged backgrounds.

The federal assistance programs for college students are composed of several separate programs: The Basic Educational Opportunity Grant program (BEOG) in 1974 granted approximately 543,000 college student awards, with an average stipend of $620 per award; the Supplemental Educational Opportunity Grant program (SEOG) granted awards to 350,000 recipients at an average stipend of $540 per awardee; the Statt Student Incentive Grant program (SSIG) granted awards to 302,000 recipients at an average stipend of $600 per awardee; the College Work-Study program (CWS granted 575,000 awards at an average stipend of $560 per recipient; the National Direct Student Loan program (NDSL) granted awards to 749,000 recipients at an average stipend of $690 per recipient; and the Guaranteed Student Loan program (GSL) granted 669,000 awards at an average loan of $1,250 per student (see Tables 8.12 and 8.13). However, the total number of students receiving federal assistance is not the sum of all of these awards because many students receive funds from several of the above categories. For example, a student might qualify for the GSL program and also for the CWS and NDSL programs. The total number of students receiving federal educational assistance through the U.S. Office of Education assistance program was 1,584,000 or 24.6 percent of the total college enrollment. About 95.2 percent of all recipients from the federal program were undergraduates and 4.8 percent were graduate students. On the other hand, many minority students pay their own college costs (see Table 8.16).

Graduate students were excluded from applying for BEOG, SEOG, and SSIG programs; however, 3.9 percent of the graduates qualified for the CWS program, 6.1 percent for the NDSL program, and 15.4 percent for the GSL program. There are no equal opportunity educational programs that provide assistance for graduate students by the federal government.

In addition to the federal assistance program operated by the U.S. Office of Education there are many state-operated assistance programs. An example of such a program is the Equal Opportunity program operated by New York State. During the 1974-75 school year the State University of New York four-year colleges granted equal opportunity grants to 8,421 students; while New York's public supported community colleges provided equal opportunity grants to 3,277 students (see Table 8.14). At New York State's four-year college campuses 76.5 percent of the equal opportunity grants went to minority students and 23.5 percent went to whites. At New York State publicly supported two-year colleges, 62.5 percent of the

TABLE 8.12

Percentage of Students Receiving Aid under Office of Education Assistance Programs,
by Selected Characteristics of Recipients, 1974-75

Characteristics	BEOG Recipients	SEOG Recipients	SSIG[a] Recipients	CWS Recipients	NDSL Recipients	GSL Recipients	Total[b] (unduplicated count)
Total	543,000	350,000	302,000	575,000	749,000	669,000	1,584,000
Percent	34.0	22.1	19.1	36.3	47.3	42.2	24.6
Ethnic group							
Minority	48.1	47.8	21.0	32.6	28.9	18.0	33.6
Nonminority	52.0	52.3	79.0	67.5	71.1	82.0	66.4
Sex							
Female	54.5	54.1	49.6	54.0	49.6	45.8	51.0
Male	45.5	45.9	50.4	46.0	50.4	54.2	49.0
Status							
Dependent undergraduates family income							
Less than $7,500	53.5	54.3	34.8	38.5	30.8	13.5	33.3
$7,500-$11,999	25.3	22.4	27.5	25.9	24.7	18.2	24.8
More than $11,999	7.3	5.3	25.2	17.2	21.4	37.3	19.1
Independent undergraduates	14.0	18.1	12.5	14.5	17.0	15.6	18.0
Graduate students	--	--	--	3.9	6.1	15.4	4.8

[a] All numbers pertaining to the SSIG recipients are inflated since many institutions were unable to report these recipients separately. The reported numbers include many students (more than half) who receive only state funds and no federal scholarship support.

[b] Excludes Guaranteed Student Loan program.

Source: American Council on Education, Student Assistance Participants and Programs 1974-75, Higher Education Panel Reports, No. 27, December 1975.

TABLE 8.13

Average Amount of Assistance Awarded under Office
of Education Assistance Programs, by Control
and Type of Institution, 1974-75
(awards rounded to nearest ten dollars)

Institutional Characteristics	BEOG	SEOG	SSIG*	CWS	NDSL	GSL
Total	620	540	600	560	690	1,250
Control						
Public	610	490	490	600	630	1,190
Private	670	660	700	510	770	1,330
Type						
Public two-year	580	400	560	610	440	970
Private two-year	680	470	770	440	790	1,740
Public four-year	640	490	480	540	600	1,180
Private four-year	660	660	710	490	730	1,280
Public university	630	610	460	700	760	1,250
Private university	660	740	630	660	930	1,390

*All numbers pertaining to the SSIG recipients are inflated since many institutions were unable to report these recipients separately. The reported numbers include many students (more than half) who receive only state funds and no federal scholarship support.

Source: American Council on Education, Student Assistance Participants and Programs 1974-75, Higher Education Panel Reports, No. 27, December 1975.

TABLE 8.14

Distribution of New York Four-Year State-Operated Campus
EOP Students, Outside of New York City, 1974-75

Race or Ethnic Background	Four-Year College		Two-Year College	
	Number	Percent	Number	Percent
Black/Negro	4,682	55.6	1,851	56.5
Native American	115	1.4	13	0.4
Asian American	96	1.4	6	0.2
Hispanic American	1,002	12.0	165	5.0
White (other than Hispanic American)	1,976	23.5	1,230	37.5
Other	550	6.5	4	0.4
Total	8,421	100.0	3,277	100.0

Source: State University of New York, The 1974-75 Annual Report of the Educational Opportunity Program (EOP), Revised (Albany, 1976).

recipients were minority students and 37.5 percent were white. The
grants include a full fellowship award for study.

It might be of interest to the reader to take a look at the sources
of income for college attendance for students who are enrolled in four-
year colleges and universities as compared to those who enroll in
two-year colleges. There are several glaring differences of income
sources available to students in the two types of institutions: among
the two-year college students 18.8 percent receive assistance from
their spouses compared to only 11.4 percent for students who attend
four-year colleges and universities; 55.8 percent of students enrolled
in the four-year colleges receive assistance from their parents compared to only 27.3 percent of those enrolled in two-year colleges;
8.0 percent of students enrolled in four-year colleges and universities receive benefits under the GI Bill of Rights compared to 16.3
percent of students enrolled in two-year colleges (see Tables 8.15
and 8.16). Further, at the four-year college level 11.4 percent of
the college students receive state scholarships or grants compared
to only 3.7 percent of those who attend two-year colleges. These
data suggest that students enrolled in two-year colleges are more
economically disadvantaged and they may expect less support from
their parents than those enrolled in four-year colleges; it also suggests that fewer two-year college students receive state scholarships;
it would also appear that many of the Vietnam War veterans who re-
turned to college enrolled in two-year colleges rather than four-year
colleges and universities.

On the other hand, Native Americans may receive financial support that is independent of the regular grant programs; many receive
support from the government through the Bureau of Indian Affairs.
In 1974, 13,895 Native American students received support from the
BIA: 13,374 were undergraduates and 521 were graduate students
(see Table 4.7).

It is clear that the phrase "equal access to higher education
for every citizen who desires it" must be backed with appropriate resources if the phrase is to have meaning. Currently, in the United
States it is those with the ability and the money who may attend college. We must see to it that those with ability and no money can attend.

PROGRAMS FOR STUDENT ASSISTANCE

Federal Programs

At all levels in higher education the federal government plays
a key role as the major source of student aid funds at both private
and public colleges. Through the Higher Education Act of 1965 and

TABLE 8.15

Percent of Undergraduate Postsecondary Students Expecting to Receive Income
from Selected Sources Between July 1973 and June 1974
and Average Amount Received

Source of Income	All Students		Four-Year College and University Students		Two-Year College Students		Vocational School Students	
	Percent of Students with Income from Specific Source	Average Amount Received	Percent of Students with Income from Specific Source	Average Amount Received	Percent of Students with Income from Specific Source	Average Amount Received	Percent of Students with Income from Specific Source	Average Amount Received
Personal savings	34.0	$742	42.6	$742	24.1	$703	20.4	$806
Earning while taking courses	44.3	3,289	39.9	2,400	52.9	3,930	46.1	4,721
Spouse's earnings	14.8	5,944	11.4	5,324	18.8	6,630	20.2	6,185
Parents	42.2	1,607	55.8	1,690	27.3	1,308	19.9	1,431
V.A. benefits	11.5	1,742	8.0	1,755	16.3	1,758	16.0	1,701
State scholarship or grant	7.9	658	11.4	707	3.7	383	(B)	(B)
Local scholarship or grant	6.9	689	10.3	712	(B)	(B)	(B)	(B)
National defense student loan	5.2	654	8.3	661	(B)	(B)	(B)	(B)
Federal guaranteed student loan	5.1	1,139	6.2	1,124	(B)	(B)	5.0	1,238

Note: (B) = Base less than 75,000.

Source: U.S. Bureau of the Census, Current Population Reports, "Income and Expenses of Students Enrolled in Postsecondary Schools: October 1973," Series P-20, No. 281 (Washington, D.C.: U.S. Government Printing Office, 1975), Table I.

TABLE 8.16

Source of Income for Postsecondary Students 16 Years Old and Over, 1973

Source of Income	All Students		Black Students		Percent Black of All Students
	Number (thousands)	Percent	Number (thousands)	Percent	
Personal savings	3,254	34	170	22	5
Earnings while taking courses	4,855	50	316	40	7
Spouse's earnings or savings	1,809	19	125	16	7
Parents	3,924	41	211	27	5
College Work-Study program	441	5	93	12	21
National Defense Student Loan	524	5	81	10	15
Educational Opportunity Grant	322	3	88	11	27
Federal guaranteed student loan program	513	5	52	7	10
Basic Educational Opportunity Grant	105	1	19	2	18
Veterans Administration benefits	1,146	12	94	12	8
Personal loan	370	4	43	5	12
State scholarship or grant	775	8	74	9	10
Local scholarship or grant	699	7	62	8	9
Social Security benefits	395	4	4	59	7
Public assistance	104	1	25	3	24
Educational expenses from employer	488	5	24	3	5
Other sources	811	8	79	10	10
Not reported	246	3	32	4	13
Total students	9,673	100	789	100	8

Source: U.S. Bureau of the Census, Current Population Reports, "The Social and Economic Status of the Black Population in the United States, 1974," Special Studies, Series P-23, No. 54 (Washington, D.C.: U.S. Government Printing Office, 1975), Table 71.

its 1972 amendments the federal government has made funds available to college students from low- and middle-income families. These funds are generally referred to as Educational Opportunity Grants. The intent of these financial aid programs is to put a college education within the grasp of every student, regardless of how poor (see Table 8.17).

The federal government's Upward Bound program is different: It was planned as a crossover program from secondary education to college, designed to prepare disadvantaged high school graduates for college work.

Initially, federal support for college training was targeted to give assistance to students whose families met the government's criteria for poverty. However, federal aid programs have been expanded to include support for students from middle-class families.

In 1975, six federal student aid programs were operational:

The Basic Educational Opportunity Grant program (BEOG) was authorized by the 1972 Education Amendments and provides direct grants to both part-time and full-time students. The maximum award is $1,400, minus some family contribution based on family income and assets; the minimum award is $200. At no time may the grant exceed one-half the actual cost of attendance (tuition and fees, room and board, books, expenses).

The Guaranteed Student Loan program (GSL) awards are made directly by the lending institutions and guaranteed by the federal government or by state agencies. Undergraduates may borrow a total of $7,500, and graduates a total of $10,000. During the repayment period, which runs between five and ten years, interest is payable at the rate of 7 percent. Interest is paid by the federal government during in-school, grace, and specified deferment periods.

The Supplemental Educational Opportunity Grant program (SEOG) has been in existence for over ten years and is one of three campus-based student aid programs. "Campus-based" means that the funds are given directly to the participating institutions which, in turn, select students with "exceptional" financial needs. The awards may be as great as one-half the total amount of student financial aid provided by the institution but may not exceed $1,500 annually.

The State Student Incentive Grant program (SSIG) was enacted under the 1972 Education Amendments and began operating in 1974-75. Appropriations are made available to participating states and territories on a 50-50 matching basis, with states agreeing to maintain previously established funding levels. Awards up to $1,500 yearly are given to undergraduates who have substantial financial need and who meet specifically defined state requirements. Because of varying accounting methods, many institutions have been unable to separate the federal SSIG money from other money; therefore, the average award reported is probably 25 percent higher than the actual.

TABLE 8.17

Number of NDSL, SEOG, and CWS Aid Recipients and Amounts Spent in
These Programs by Racial/Ethnic Distribution, Fiscal Year 1974

Race or Ethnic Group	Unduplicated Total		NDSL		SEOG		CWS	
	Number	Percent	Number	Percent	Number	Percent	Number	Percent
Negro/Black	284,321	26.9	170,778	25.8	143,521	38.1	147,746	27.4
Native American	8,563	0.8	4,194	0.6	4,697	1.2	3,641	0.7
Asian American	11,423	1.1	6,839	1.0	4,498	1.2	6,368	1.2
Hispanic American	74,594	7.1	38,969	5.9	36,560	9.7	40,074	7.4
White (other than Hispanic American)	604,051	57.1	388,447	58.8	165,276	43.9	304,022	56.3
All other students in programs	74,541	7.0	51,530	7.8	22,001	5.8	37,701	7.0
Total	1,057,493	100.0	660,757	100.0	376,553	100.0	539,552	100.0

Source: U.S. Office of Education, Office of Student Assistance, BPE Division of Student Support and Special Programs, Program Support Branch, unpublished, 1976.

The College Work-Study program (CWS) provides part-time, on- and off-campus jobs to students. Under this campus-based financial aid program created in 1964, institutions receive funds to pay 80 percent of the wages of students working in either public or nonprofit organizations. Students must be enrolled at least half time, and their earnings are limited to an amount no greater than the difference between their assessed financial need and the amount of other financial aid.

The National Direct Student Loan program (NDSL), the oldest of the aid programs, was enacted in 1958 as the National Defense Student Loan Program. Participating institutions provide 10 percent matching funds for this low-interest (3 percent), campus-based loan program. There is a ten-year repayment period. Up to 100 percent of the loan may be canceled if the borrower takes a teaching job in an economically deprived area or teaches the handicapped; up to 50 percent of the loan may be canceled if the borrower serves in the armed forces in an area of hostilities. This loan program enables a student to borrow money directly from a savings and loan association, credit union, bank, or other lender. Each state handles the program differently.

A New York State Program

The State University of New York (not including New York City) Educational Opportunity program (EOP) was designed to increase higher education opportunities for the state's economically and educationally disadvantaged population (Blair 1975). It had its roots in the City University of New York College Discovery program, established in 1965, and the State University of New York Full Opportunity program, established at most state-operated and community colleges across the state in 1970. New York State was selected as an example of state college aid programs for the disadvantaged. Aggregate data on total U.S. state programs are not available.

In 1969 a similar program, the Higher Educational Opportunity program (HEOP), was established to aid the involvement of private colleges and universities of the state in this type of special effort. The New York State Equal Opportunity legislation requires the basic funding of the Educational Opportunity program be on two bases: state-operated campuses receive funds for each EOP student for special supportive services, while community college EOPs are funded only for direct student costs. The program also requires that students meet both criteria of disadvantageness--economic and educational--in order to qualify for support, a definite weakness. High-achieving, academically poor students cannot get support.

The State University of New York Educational Opportunity program included 53 campuses of the State University of New York. Of these EOP campuses, 25 were local community colleges. State-operated EOP campuses reported a total 1974-75 EOP student enrollment of approximately 7,400. This enrollment was made possible through a state legislature appropriation of $9,591,000 for state-operated EOP campuses. Program projections indicate that there was enrollment of about 8,000 EOP students on state-operated campuses during 1975-76 year.

In New York State it would appear that the Educational Opportunity program on state-operated campuses is carrying out its prime mission of making expanded and viable higher educational opportunities available to some disadvantaged students (economically disadvantaged, but high-achieving students are excluded) that are traditionally bypassed by institutions of higher education. A total of 77.5 percent of first-time 1974-75 state-operated campus EOP students had high school averages below a B.

Without EOP or similar programs, most of these 1974-75 students would most likely not have gained admittance to college or possibly even tried to go to college or seek any significant amount of education beyond the high school level.

The report of the EOP of the State University drawn from the records of a total of 7,756 state-operated campus EOP students who have persisted in the program up to ten or more semesters through the end of 1974-75 shows that of the total of those who attended up to eight semesters (four years) 5,103 (65.8 percent) progressed at the "expected" rate. State-operated campuses reported that a total of only 1,584 students transferred or dropped out of the program. Further, a total of only 41.4 percent of these were reported as leaving the program for academic reasons.

In 1975 New York State-operated EOP campuses reported expending a total of $16,245,796 for Educational Opportunity Program: 45 percent came from state EOP funds, 17.5 percent came from their own operating budgets, and 37.5 percent came from federal and other sources. There is a trend on state campuses that EOP students must be dependent on sources other than state EOP funding. These other funding sources are often less accessible to EOP students which may ultimately cause some to leave college.

9

MINORITY STUDENTS
ON CAMPUS

Minorities are no longer the invisible people on college campuses, but appear to the general public to be flooding our colleges
and universities. Open enrollment policies as well as increased
scholarships and expanded higher educational opportunities for minority students within recent years sharply raised minority enrollment,
but as the Ford Foundation study found, enrollment among minorities
"will have to exceed that of whites for some time before they achieve
representation corresponding to their proportion within the population" (Stent and Brown 1974). Within the United States, historically
and up until the present time, minority students have had to isolate
themselves culturally, educationally, and socially in an effort to
assure their cultural survival. Within the last decade minority students have become increasingly aware of the great importance of
higher education in their struggle for justice, survival, and a better
life. They have learned the great value of power that is achieved
through voting and have become active politically.

Minority students have aspired to those professions which here-
tofore have seen virtually none of their members involved. In highly
specialized fields such as banking, metallurgy, engineering, international relations, and diplomacy, their representation is uniformly low.
Minority students have seen the beginnings of their own businesses,
and, in fact, they are beginning to flourish. They have witnessed
the beginnings of separate institutions of higher education for the Native Americans and for Chicanos.* Teacher education has recognized

---

*"Chicano" is used in many instances to refer to a person of
Mexican American origin. The term is not used to refer to other
Hispanic Americans.

the richness of bilingual-bicultural studies and minority students are
taking courses related to their cultural heritage.

THE EFFECTS OF STUDENT UNREST IN THE 1960S

The mid-1960s saw an unusual phenomenon. Colleges and
universities were in the midst of a variety of highly publicized disturbances. The types of protest ranged from institutional disciplin-
ary action, changes in major institutional programs such as the development and facilities for ethnic studies programs, to breaking
into and wrecking buildings; marching, picketing, and rallying; and
interrupting college and university functions such as classes, speeches,
and meetings, to general campus strikes. There were instances of
boycotting of classes as well as the extremes of people being injured
and killed which occurred at Kent State and Jackson State colleges.
Private universities, highly selective institutions with often barely
token black representation, and institutions with large enrollments
were those which were far more likely to have campus disturbances
(Hodgkinson 1970; Astin and Bayer 1971).

Campus revolts became the first great protest of modern
times against the academic community at large. It was a protest being applied by Third World students who were clamoring for education which was relevant to their life styles, aspirations, and goals.
It was a protest against U.S. colleges and universities which were
continuing to be places where the professor's education might continue, but where the black student's education might not start. It
was a protest against the bachelor's degree, master's degree, and
the doctoral credit card which had been validated by the white ghost
of previous centuries and universally accepted as criteria of excel-
lence in the twentieth century; it was a protest against the Cambodian
invasion and what many considered an immoral war; and against the
continued pollution of the world's environmental resources; and finally it was a protest against education which never touched the lives of
black Third World students.

Many viewed the rebellions and riots as manifestations of
"black power," which the majority population indiscriminately linked
to crime in the streets, poverty, slums, and the civil rights movement. There is a manifest danger that the campus unrest of the
1960s will be all too easily dismissed as merely a passing phase;
but the destiny of the U.S. university has already been greatly af-
fected and changed by this period of unrest. These revolts represented a major attack for change on higher education; an attack which
was well deserved from the point of view of black people.

The way that the university and college world does recoup and respond to the call for change will depend a great deal upon the representation of black students on its campuses. Unfortunately, the picture of black students' experiences in institutions of higher education is a zig-zag one. Although black enrollment has increased, so has total college enrollment in the United States. Relatively few black students graduate, because their drop-out rate is high. This results from deeply embedded institutionalized racism, poor high school preparation, inadequate financial aid, and lack of counseling and remedial instruction for black students.

The late 1960s were unique in that they marked both the climax and the signal for the folding of the civil rights movement on college campuses. Much of the initial impetus for open admissions, curriculum change, the recognition of exclusionary curriculum materials, and the ethnic studies programs of the 1970s grew out of black student pressures.

Examining the university crisis in the past decade of student unrest is an analysis of dissonance, for the colleges and universities are no longer the social, ivory-tower groups they were previously. "As long as the university represented a relative homogenous student population which mirrored the melting pot Caucasian system in which students thought they wished to live could it represent a cohesive design for living" (Ballard 1973).

A REALIGNMENT OF PRIORITIES IN THE 1970S?

The university of today will never return to the bimodal approach to racial problems which purported to be color-blind in its commitment to integration, or to the dependence upon traditionally discipline-oriented methods of inquiry. Undergraduate education, as well as some graduate specialties, will take place outside of the university: in industry, within the ghettos, in socioeconomic agencies and cultural institutions.

The emergence of black and brown faces reflected in the increased enrollment in colleges that previously had made little attempt to encourage their attendance was coupled with a peak and beginning decline in student financial aid funds between 1968 and 1970. The ensuing severe recession and national cutbacks of all grants within the nation's colleges and universities has greatly influenced the university environment and caused a rethinking of priorities by administrators and faculty. The result has been that continuing efforts of minority students to make the environment more hospitable to them have met with increasing hostility and resistance.

The sudden immediacy of the civil rights movement was the
assertion by Afro-Americans of their right to the same educational,
economic, and political benefits enjoyed by the majority white population. From this auspicious beginning, a multiplier effect occurred;
as we now see the Puerto Rican and Chicano groups leading the fight
for bilingualism as an asset rather than a liability. Social justice and
equal educational opportunity as treasured American concepts for the
student were set in a new mold by blacks who asserted that they must
take on real meaning in practice. Each ethnic group responded educationally and politically to the contemporary demand for equality of
opportunity, constitutional protection, and education which was meaningful and relevant. College campuses were urged to reflect this
multiethnic pluralism in all aspects of their functioning. Nevertheless, blacks and Hispanic Americans remain underrepresented in
colleges and universities, although their numbers increased on the
campuses within the last decade. It is shocking that so few Third
World students received bachelor's degrees or advanced degrees in
the last decade. The doors have opened, but it appears that the student suffocates before he finds the exits.

Colleges and universities within this country have always represented the major focal point in the developing struggle for equal
educational opportunity and social justice. Access to higher education becomes the most strategic and significant point to analyze the
effectiveness of education as the major tool for upward social mobility. For every other ethnic group within our society except for
minority groups that are not white, education has been the first rung
on the ladder to later success.

Third World students on our campuses have not succumbed to
the traditional assimilation attitude of previous student generations.
They have negated assimilation. They have maintained through their
dress, through their strong identification with campus ethnic groups
that there is more than one legitimate way of learning without paying
the penalties of second-class citizenship. The obvious determination
by blacks, Chicanos, Puerto Ricans, Asian Americans and Native
Americans to reject educational integration and accommodation has
been based on their experience, and the experience of their parents
in the United States. This experience includes the minute historical
pace of desegregation of public schools and universities, the apathy
toward affirmative action, as well as the incredible scarcity of Native American, Chicano, and black scholars among the leaders and
academic elite of our society: such as professors, deans, and administrators. In the U.S. university, integration has too often assumed that nonwhite students had to be inculcated with prevailing
white values and brainwashing before they could be "truly" educated
in the transmitted tradition of U.S. culture. Doctoral degrees in all

fields have often been as much the high degree of competence as they have been the "patience" to endure and overcome the hurdles of institutionalized racism. For the historically underprivileged black and other minority students the question of success in higher education has now become more than just the mere question of obtaining a degree for admission into American life.

ENROLLMENT AND RETENTION

Student leaders, civil rights groups, and those who were vocal about the dynamics of the policy changes of the 1960s were consistent in advocating a goal in enrollment for blacks, Puerto Ricans, Asian Americans, and Native Americans in proportion to their representation in the population. Nowhere near this representation has been accomplished. A projection of education statistics to 1982 based on 1974 data of entering college freshmen indicates that minority black undergraduate enrollment will not reach parity with the white population by 1978 (USOE 1975).

A study of black students in white colleges by Boyd (1974) indicated that black students are primarily graduates of public high schools who go to school in their home area. They attend and participate in classes at least as much as other students and maintain at least a C average. The data indicate that they usually obtain adequate help with their problems by using some combination of the resources available to them on the campus. The most difficult problem is perceived to be obtaining sufficient funds to finance their education. High school preparation is also cited as a critical problem. In spite of charges at many predominantly white colleges of preferential treatment, almost 70 percent feel that their college does not really care about having black students on the campus. They feel that in the area of special academic help they receive none. While 79 percent of those who receive no academic help feel that they need none, 76 percent of those who receive it feel that it is adequate. Interestingly, the Boyd study documents the reactions of the majority (59 percent) of black students to intense competition as being motivational and increasing self-confidence and ability to function. Similarly, 64 percent feel that they have no ability to influence college programs. This has less negative impact than it might, because 57 percent feel that black students can influence college programs through organized group effort.

Financial security is an overwhelming and constant burden for black students. The principal source of money for two-thirds of black students in the Boyd study were on loans and scholarships, and almost 75 percent supplemented their income by working. Scholar-

ships, loans, and grants are rarely given to part-time students.
Therefore, the majority of black students must work or accumulate
funds before enrolling in college. These combined factors relate to
the longer length of time required for black students to obtain degrees and their tendency to be somewhat older than white students.

The tradition in higher education for qualifying for scholarships
(usually given as loans) is in most instances determined by a needs
assessment. Under this arrangement, the issue of equitable financial distribution works to the disadvantage of black, Puerto Rican,
and Native American students, as the complicated and lengthy forms
usually must be filled out by the student as well as his parent. For
Third World parents who have not attended college and are in most
need of financial aid, the complexity of these forms as they relate to
an accurate picture of family income results in underapportionment
of scholarship aid. Black families have by and large only recently
arrived at the income level indicated and they must spend more to
remain there. This is particularly true of blacks who attend institutions located in urban areas with the consequence of higher costs of
living.

The major target population of many federal funding programs
has been low income students. This federal funding has declined and
the pressure for higher education to expand its previous commitment
to black Third World students has generally been reduced from the
prodigious efforts of the 1960s. Gains in the numbers of blacks and
Hispanic Americans attending college in the United States did occur,
but these gains were slight and their representation in higher education is still disastrously lower than their representation in the population. On the other hand, the impact of this increase in enrollment
was significant.

We will now turn our attention to the two largest minority
groups: blacks and Chicanos. We selected these two groups for
special attention because of their size and visibility on campus. We
will also discuss life on community college campuses because they
enroll such a high percentage of minority students.

BLACK STUDENTS ON CAMPUS

The position of a black student at a predominantly white college compared with one in a black college is a study in contrast. We
will examine certain aspects of student life: tutoring and social life,
the effect of financial situation on social life, the ability to effect
change, admittance into graduate schools, and minority programs.
These views are based on the personal experiences of the authors
and from small group sessions with students and faculty members
from black and white colleges.

Tutoring and Social Life

Many black college students enter with poor high school preparation, due largely to poor counseling and instruction, especially
those who attend poor ghetto high schools. This poor preparation
forces the black student to seek remedial help if he is to survive
academically. The need for remedial help at white institutions may
indirectly contribute to student failure. Black students frequently
have to set aside portions of their day for tutoring in addition to time
for regular study and social activities. The result is that the black
student on a white campus often will decide to skip desperately needed
tutoring in order to socialize so that he can feel a part of campus life.
This decision usually results in academic failure.

Even though the need for tutoring on black college campuses is
the same, time needed to socialize is not as great, because of the
availability of large numbers of blacks. Also, because those who
are tutored are black, black students may feel welcome; whereas,
on a white campus, an all-black tutoring session would cause many
blacks to drop out.

Black students attending college close to home also have social
pressure exerted on them by other noncollege blacks. The college
student is afraid of becoming a social outcast and is forced to make
time in his busy schedule to socialize with his old social group.
Often many members of his high school group are not college students and cannot understand why he cannot continue to "hang out"
with them.

Finance and Social Life

Many black students must work to meet their financial obliga-
tions. Still, most of these students do not have sufficient funds to
own a car or to have "pocket money." Thus, black students have to
depend heavily on public transportation for both inter- and intracity
commuting. This often occurs at times when social activities are
held off campus. Many social activities may not get in full swing
until around midnight, but the student must leave before the party
really gets going to catch the last bus home or to the campus. Sometimes the students are the victims of verbal ridicule.

Ability to Effect Change

Blacks at white colleges are not able to affect college activities
as easily as their counterparts at black colleges because blacks have
little control over the student government. Blacks may be elected to

offices at white colleges with considerable white support. On white campuses blacks must depend on whites who are sympathetic toward blacks in order to get the student government to make a few concessions; these concessions must be zealously guarded, because when funds are short, they are usually taken away.

The inability of black students to effect change by themselves may be translated into having to live with choices made by white students. For example, the student government may appropriate funds for a performance by Three Dog Night, Led Zeppelin, or the Dave Clark Five and reject funds for performances by Muddy Waters or Isaac Hayes. This situation is usually reversed at black colleges.

Food selection at white colleges is said to be made to provide students with a balanced diet. Yet, the selection is made with a complete disregard for black food choices. However, black colleges are able to offer ethnic foods that produce a balanced diet. The difference in offerings is largely attributed to majority status in the two situations.

Black students at white colleges are unable to participate in many of the decision-making processes, while at black colleges they have control of the student government and get appointed to the influential university committees where policies are being formed. The ability to participate in student government and to aid in shaping future directions for academic institutions could be one reason why the black colleges have produced more outstanding national and international black leaders. White colleges have not been able to produce individuals comparable to Booker T. Washington, Robert Russa Morton, W. E. B. DuBois, James Weldon Johnson, Mary McLeod Bethune, John Hope Franklin, Ira Reid, Patricia Harris, James M. Nabrit, and Martin Luther King.

Admittance into Graduate Schools

The black colleges account for more than 75 percent of the bachelor's degrees earned by blacks. However, most black college graduates apply for graduate studies at white colleges. The black college students who graduate in the top quarter of the class usually have little difficulty in getting admitted to graduate schools, which have a long tradition of seeking or considering academically superior blacks for their programs. The black college graduates not in the top quarter of their class are only slightly considered for acceptance, but usually denied admittance. White colleges usually fail to look at the overall picture of the black graduate applying for an advanced degree. White institutions tend to look solely at grade-point averages; and they also tend to look down on the academic quality of black colleges. Graduate schools have not adjusted their graduate admission policies to realize that a black graduate with a grade-point average of 2.6 (on the 4.0 system) who worked 30 or even 40 hours per week is probably capable of greater achievement than the student who finished his undergraduate education with a 3.0 and did not have to work for pocket money.

Minority Programs

Minority programs at white colleges were initiated to maintain tranquility on campus during the years of turbulent riots and unrest, while black colleges looked at minority programs as a means for bringing more underprivileged individuals into the American mainstream of life. Black colleges staffed their programs with competent dedicated individuals who desired to see the programs succeed. Many white institutions viewed minority programs as mere federal mandates.

Two very interesting methods were used to try to insure the failure of minority programs at white colleges. One method was to (knowingly) hire incompetent individuals to staff the program or competent individuals who did not wish to see the programs succeed. The incompetent were overt in their bungling and decision errors. Their best efforts were not adequate enough to produce success. The competent were more covert and subtle in their actions. They took advantage of the minority's weak educational background and their strong desire to be accepted as another student on campus. These competents would counsel the minority student to register for the most difficult combination of courses and instructors so that the minority student would quickly flunk out of school, to be replaced by an even weaker student academically, who in turn would flunk out. It is not unusual to find minority students with deficiencies in reading, writing, and mathematics registered in regular freshman calculus, physics, and chemistry in the same semester. This type of counseling has been used to produce data to document failure of minority programs and to justify allocating the funds to more traditional units of the white university.

Another method used by predominantly white institutions is that of funding the minority program inadequately. With this method, administrators deliberately hold back funds so that ineffective operation of the program is assured. Once failure is irreversible, the necessary funds are released, making it possible for the college to say that the entire appropriation was spent and the result was a failure.

Some problems are faced by blacks regardless of the institutions they attend. They do not shape their own educational destiny. The academic and residential activities of blacks at white institutions are directly under the control of white administrators. The educational destiny of blacks at black institutions (public and private) is also controlled by whites; even though college personnel are predominantly black, they must respond to a board of trustees that is predominantly white or a board whose most influential members are white. The administrators of public black institutions are predominantly black, but they must adhere to policies determined by white government officials. Moreover, programs for blacks must be accredited by predominantly white agencies.

THE CHICANO STUDENT IN THE 1970S

The college campus is often perceived by Chicano students as something akin to a foreign country. While the Chicano community is certainly in constant flux, and while higher education expectancy is not nearly as alien as it was five years ago, a Chicano student can normally be characterized as one who had not always planned to go to a college or university before his senior year in high school.

The social distance between the Chicano student and the rest of the college campus is far greater than whatever distances were present in secondary school. Under most circumstances the Chicano student is in a far greater numerical minority than he was in high school. Moreover, if the Chicano college student is one who has had to move away from home the alienation is intensified. The average Chicano student lives in a neighborhood that is predominantly Chicano and very often goes to a high school that has a significant number of Chicano students. When he goes to college, the proportion of Chicano students as well as the absolute number is small; the total number of students is most often larger; and very often the Chicano student will be living in an area that is predominantly Anglo. This places an added burden of adjustment on the Chicano student.

Little empirical data is available on Chicano undergraduates in the United States. From the literature that is available, some conclusions about the climate experienced by Chicanos on campuses, as well as some of their stated problems are much the same as for other minority groups. Finances are a determining factor in attending college. Using California as an example, the state's Mexican Americans have a substantially lower per capita income than Anglos and other ethnic groups within the community. Usually the bases for selecting a college were money and distance from home. Certainly the physical location of a college is closely interrelated with finances, and it is easy to see why this becomes the student's most important consideration in college selection.

As Lopez and Enos (1972 p. 26) report, although

> many Chicano parents are reluctant to approve of
> their children moving away from home, there are,
> of course, a good many reasons for this. . . .
> Too many people, both in high schools and in col-
> leges (counselors, recruiters, etc.) stereotype
> all Chicanos in this category. It is not unusual to
> hear people talk of the difficulty they had convincing
> parents to allow their youngsters to move away
> from home, and this is an especially common ex-
> pression as it refers to young women. While it
> must be conceded that this parental concern is
> more prominent among Chicanos than it is among
> the rest of the community, it is by no means a
> universal attitude. It is in fact a minority of
> Chicano parents who strongly resist the idea of
> their children going away to college. However,
> because of the difficulty this attitude has some-
> times caused and because this parental attitude
> is not as visible among black and Anglo students,
> it is often assumed to be near universal for
> Chicanos.

Parental concern is easily understood when one realizes that the Chicano parent is already anxious about the possibilities of future success for his son or daughter. They have every reason not to trust the educational institution. They have heard stories about discrimination, drugs, student demonstrations, and violence. They have read magazines and newspapers and are often very concerned about American sexual activities as indicated by the press and the continuing and changing patterns of coed dormitories. Perhaps most importantly they know from experience that college attendance must be tremendously expensive, and they have to face the problems of going into debt.

The problems confronting the Chicano community with getting into and graduating from college are probably best stated by Lopez and Enos (1972):

> The relative absence of Chicanos as graduate stu-
> dents in our colleges and universities is the final
> stage in the vicious cycle of the educational under-
> representation of Chicanos which is self-reinforcing,

and not apt to change without tremendous effort on
the part of policymakers. The first stage of the
cycle begins in high school, where the Chicano
student often suffers the "disadvantages" of speaking mixed Spanish-English, or English with a
Spanish accent. It is continued in high school
through the influence of peers "going nowhere" who
often attempt to keep their friends from going on to
college. The pressures of the family, their financial needs, the frequent parental desire to keep
Chicanos near the home, and the cost of higher education also are part of this cycle discouraging the
Chicano student from going on to college. And then,
even if the desire to attend college develops, the
Chicano student must often survive the depressing
effects of ignorant counselors or college recruiters
who just do not have the time to see them all individually.

The cycle enters the next stage when those
few Chicano students who do go on to college enter
the white world of the average college campus.
Computerized and bureaucratic admissions and
enrollment are frustrating to any person, particularly one who doubts whether he belongs on a college campus at all. Finally, there is the shortage
of financial aid and other student support services,
all working to make the collegiate experience a
negative one for Chicano students.

It is little wonder that so few Chicano students
enter graduate school. And yet, if we are to change
the educational systems experienced by the Chicano
prior to graduate school, if the Chicano community
is to continue to advance educationally, then Chicanos with advanced degrees must be produced in
ever greater numbers. The Chicano community
needs highly educated members of La Raza so that
its self-advancement can continue to grow. However, if the past repeats itself, the Anglo-dominated
institutions will continue to decide how many Chicanos will be educated, and how educated they will be.

COMMUNITY COLLEGES: THE INFLATION
SPIRAL IN HIGHER EDUCATION

One of the most highly debated topics in higher education today
is the future of the community colleges. The charge of whether they

are evolving into "the coming slums of higher education" (Corcoran
1973) or the vehicle for equal opportunity for all does not obscure
empirical data of continued minority underrepresentation in these
colleges. When ratios are made that relate college enrollment of
blacks and Hispanic Americans to their proportion in the general
population, the picture is dismal. Interestingly, the representation
of the minorities that we do have is heavily concentrated in two-year
and four-year colleges. White undergraduates on the other hand are
found in most significant numbers at the universities.

For example, in California, of all students in public higher
education, 55 percent attended community colleges (Lopez and Enos
1972). It is clear from this study that Chicanos have a 15 percent
greater possibility of attending a community college than any of the
other public higher educational institutions in California. The glaring underrepresentation of Chicanos in higher education in this state
is even more obvious when one considers the fact that Chicanos are
at least 16 percent of the population in California. Their enrollment
in public colleges and universities of the state is only slightly above
3 percent of the total student population in the system and 5.4 percent in the state university and college system; the major representation is within the community colleges' population, 7 percent (Lopez
and Enos 1972).

Malcolm X, Martin Luther King, Navajo, Hostos, and other
names of community colleges in the United States remind us of their
intended role as comprehensive culturally pluralistic colleges. An
outgrowth of the GI Bill of Rights, these colleges of the past two
decades bear little resemblance to their few antecedents of the early
1900s; now almost all of our major cities have community colleges.
In 1970 there were more than 1,000 junior and community colleges
which enrolled more than 2 million students, and the Carnegie Commission on Higher Education has called for 500 more by 1976.

Pros and Cons

The thin veil separating the advocates of community colleges
and their severest critics is often blown about when Gleazer (1970,
p. 51), while stating that "our educational job is to do what other institutions will not or cannot do," goes on to say,

> we should be drawing many more students from the
> lower half of the academic ability scales and the
> socioeconomic measures. According to a study in
> Illinois based on 1967 data, the percentages of stu-
> dents drawn from the lower half of either of these

population groups has not increased. This, despite
the fact that 85 percent of the population of that
state is now in a junior college district and that
more than 100,000 students in those districts are
enrolled in junior colleges.

Critics of the community colleges argue that community colleges are failing the students who most need direction, order, goals
and purpose.

Jencks (1968, p. 38) and Devall (1971) spoke negatively about
community colleges ever achieving equality of educational opportunity, and they see little hope or reason for the existence of these
colleges.

Moore (1970) in Against the Odds, describes the plight of the
low-achieving community college student by noting that the total experience of attendance is often a traumatic, frustrating one. The
student knows he is not wanted.

Community college proponents (Rouche and Kirk 1973; Medsker
and Tillery 1968; and Gleazer 1970) are enthusiastic about the open-
door concept but still warn that this open door is still revolving.
They point out that through deliberate planning a large percentage of
college-age young people in this country now enter higher education
through the community college; they indicate that a continuum between
high school and the community colleges is needed in order to fulfill
the promise of the open door.

Rouche and Kirk (1973) point out that there are community colleges that have developed imaginative approaches to curricula. Studies
of "successful" programs in five community colleges which had been in
operation for at least three years led Rouche and Kirk (1973) to conclude that "community colleges can design and implement successful
programs for non-traditional, high-risk students. The present in-
vestigation not only documents that such students can be retained for
several semesters but further contends that students achieve, learn
and develop positive attitudes toward the colleges and in its developmental program."

Corcoran's (1973) essay on community colleges articulates a
concept of social justice which must be pivotal to any true assessment of the development of community colleges, a concept which
should be developed in terms of specific strategies. Social justice
in and of itself means to each the same; as a goal in this country it
has for minorities usually meant less and of inferior quality. Social
justice in higher education requires making up for past injustices as
well as the truly same opportunity to learn. The question of whether
American minorities--those who are black and brown--will find that
their degrees are of no value, and that they are still potentially power-
less, should be of first-order priority in higher education.

Marjorie R. Fallows (1975) writes accurately to the intensely personal experiences of the community college teacher as well as the student. She relates her 13 years of experience in teaching at a community college.

> When the community college student views the future, he is aware that his veneer of self-confidence is thin in comparison with that of students who graduated from more prestigious colleges. His anxiety is shared by his teachers who urged him on and taught him to believe in himself, but sometimes wonder whether they have created a marginal/modular being who will not be content with the jobs his parents hold, and will be insecure in the world to which the college has introduced him. Playing Pygmalion with one's students is a calculated risk. . . . It is a risk we have taken nationally without fully foreseeing the consequences of the open door college.

Guidance and Counseling

The Carnegie Commission mentioned in 1973 that one major problem for higher education was to create an environment for developmental growth (Carnegie Commission 1973, p. 1). This lofty goal is espoused, but for the minority student it is nevertheless obscured when the collision between purpose and procedure are pinpointed. The paucity of minority faculty in institutions of higher education is felt perhaps most keenly in the area of guidance and counseling. It would appear from the works of Erickson (1975), Rist (1970), and Karabel (1972) that the counseling or gatekeeping functions of these faculty members are key to understanding the dynamics of the junior/community college environment. These researchers reemphasize a continuing complaint of minority students that they often feel "they" are failing, "they" are the ones at fault, never the institutions.

Karabel (1972) comments on the processing of students whom society defines as marginal (lower class, white ethnics, and Third World students being usually overrepresented in this category), and notes the consequent redirection toward alternative goals which are usually of lower social rank. Karabel states that

> shared communication styles seem to influence not only the ease with which an interaction proceeds but the ability of the participants to read each other

accurately. Accuracy is particularly important in
the counseling situation where it is often inappropriate for a counselor or a student to deal with
problems explicitly, and especially inappropriate
to do so if the counselor and student are pan-
ethnically or racially different. For example, if
a white ethnic counselor thought a black or Chicano
student's major courses would not transfer to a
four-year college, it was very unlikely that he
would say so directly. Because he feared being
perceived as sending global messages that Third
World Students (T.W.S.) were not capable of fin-
ishing a four-year college, the counselor tended
not to deal with specific problems. Similarly, the
student could not say "I think your advice is non-
sense and I refuse to follow it." Both counselor
and student rely heavily on implicit cues, and the
more ethnically different they are the more implicit the cues become. Even the manner in which
advice is given--grudgingly, with many reservations, routinely or with encouragement--can function as an implicit message about the nature of
society, the student's place in it and the counselor's attitude toward the student.

It would appear from the detailed interview from the Lopez
(1972) report that the majority of Chicano students planning to attend
college and who speak to a guidance counselor or teacher are indeed
encouraged to go the community college route. It is a logical conclusion that if more minority guidance counselors were appointed on
a secondary level and particularly the community college level, this
overwhelming problem and tension which it entails for the minority
student would be lessened. Lopez and Enos (1972) say,

Chicanos, particularly students, asserted again
and again that more Chicano faculty and staff were
necessary if the institutions are ever to effectively
accept Chicanos on campus. The Chicano students
acknowledge that it does not necessarily follow that
a Chicano staff member is better able to relate to
them, but the probability that this is so is much
higher than otherwise.

Summary and Conclusions

For the many black and brown faces on our campuses, community colleges have meant hope and expanding access to higher education. They have been popularized as providing the keystone of strength for future generations through mass public higher education, as well as providing countless alternatives to the B.A. and B.S. degrees. Along with these plaudits, the not-so-subtle realities of what they are becoming are beginning to affect the total structure of student life and higher education. Suddenly the black and brown faces find that the promise of "transfer with full credit" to four-year colleges and universities of the state is often the possibility and not the actuality. The dreams and sacrifices of so many minority students and their families for higher education within our community colleges is abruptly ending in terminal occupational programs. Jobs which formerly required only basic technical education or apprenticeships—such as radiological, clinical, and laboratory technicians—now more often than not require the Associate of Arts degree (A.A.). Attrition rates and labels of second-class institutions and the slums of higher education are becoming all too prevalent.

Minorities again find themselves cogged and compromised in the wheel of educational change. The implied promise of the open door to higher education is apparently only another delusion and myth for blacks and Hispanic Americans to swallow. The argument that these institutions are in close proximity to where students live, that they stimulate and encourage high educational aspiration, and that they have become the instruments for expanding access with equal opportunity for all is blatantly untrue for Third World students. The minority students, so often channelled to the community colleges, must face the fact that these colleges are unwilling to provide fulfilling, effective programs for the so-called disadvantaged high-risk student. Nevertheless, he is counseled, propagandized, and urged to take advantage of this democratizing of U.S. higher education.

If the community colleges become increasingly the institutions for the high-risk, economically disadvantaged minorities of this country, a differential society, wherein minorities will have to prove the merit of these institutions, is perpetuated. This is beginning to occur and the states as well as the federal government and higher education must begin to seriously weigh and balance the facts, values, assumptions, and future of the community colleges. The question becomes how to enhance and perpetuate those characteristics which provide for an egalitarian, accessible, high-quality, low-cost opportunity for higher education without the sacrifice of status and quality of educational services. The promised open-door policy cannot become another revolving door only to dreams of

154 MINORITIES IN HIGHER EDUCATION

upward social and economic mobility. In this country today we hear
the voices of minority students and many educators insisting that
these colleges primarily serve the middle class, the suburban areas,
and offer too many remedial courses and poor counseling; these com-
plaints cannot be ignored.

Two-year colleges are process variables designed to cool off
society's demand for increased representation in higher education
while at the same time insuring continued limited output; that is,
an earned degree. Thus, we refer to "the inflation spiral" in higher
education: that is, minorities have increased their numbers on
campus but their relative graduation rate from college has remained
constant.

10

SUMMARY
AND RECOMMENDATIONS

Minorities are severely underrepresented in institutions of higher education in the United States at all levels: undergraduate, graduate, and professional (law, medicine, and dentistry). The most severely underrepresented minority groups are blacks and Hispanic Americans, but Native Americans and Asian Americans are also underrepresented.

For Native Americans we state our case on the underrepresentation despite the fact that some of our data might show otherwise. We feel that the Native American population in this country is larger than that indicated by the U.S. Bureau of the Census. We have found that in certain areas and states there are almost as many college students as there are Native American residents in those states as counted by the Census Bureau.

We also conclude that Asian Americans are underrepresented in institutions of higher education despite data which indicate that the percentage of Asian Americans in higher education is larger than their representation in the general population. Asian Americans are underrepresented because of the higher percentage of Asian American high school graduates and the high standing of those graduates in their high school graduating classes. Also at the graduate level, based upon the large percentage of Asian Americans who complete undergraduate studies, they are underrepresented.

Minorities are also underrepresented in the status institutions within higher education, namely, prestigious universities and four-year colleges. Generally minorities are overrepresented in two-year colleges and in lower-status four-year colleges.

Given our findings we feel compelled to make recommendations to correct the situation. Our recommendations are based on the following assumptions: First, higher education is a national

concern and should be dealt with first at the national level. We feel
that higher education is necessary for the general welfare of the
country, and that the federal government should take the initial action to correct this situation. Ours is a very mobile society where
students trained in an institution of higher education in one state
frequently move to another state; thus, the responsibility for higher
education at the state level is less clear in correcting social injustices. Second, every qualified person should have an equal chance
to compete for a college education regardless of his financial cir-
cumstance due largely to accidents of birth. That is, a country that
values social justice and the development of its human resources
should provide a poor black or Puerto Rican student from Harlem
with the same chance to compete for a college education as wealthy
parents from Scarsdale generally provide for their children. The
fact that one child was born into a poor family and another into a
wealthy family should not be the major criterion for getting a college
education. Nevertheless, given the current status of affairs in the
United States, the college attendance is highly correlated with money
available to students. Even attendance at a quality elementary and
high school is highly correlated with family income. The right of
every child to become whatever he is capable of should be a national
policy of this country. In this country the child who dreams of becoming president of the United States, a banker, a state governor,
an airline pilot, an astronaut, a teacher, or a football coach will not
have those dreams become reality without a college education. Third,
we assume that incentive-type legislation (and appropriations) at the
federal level must be forthcoming in order to produce greater equity
in the allocation of higher educational opportunities among all racial
groups in the United States. Fourth, we make the basic assumption
that the availability pool for undergraduate education--minority high
school graduates--must be increased in order to increase minority
undergraduate enrollment. Fifth, the availability pool for graduate
work must also be increased in order to increase the number of
minority graduate student enrollment. Sixth, student aid formulas
can be adjusted to give every qualified student a chance to attend college. Seventh, incentives can be provided by the federal government
to stimulate curricula reform at our colleges and universities.
Eighth, special attention can be given to the bilingual educational
concerns of students from bilingual backgrounds, such as the experiences of many Hispanic American and Asian American students.
Ninth, special efforts can be made to enroll minority students in the
critical professions that are now without even a minimum minority
representation, such as anthropology, educational psychology, nuclear medicine, and geology. Tenth, efforts can be made to coordinate federal, state, and local administration of equal opportunity

programs. Eleventh, college aid programs can take the form of grants rather than loans. Loans will just insure that the economically disadvantaged person will remain so after graduation with the government as the creditor. The economically advantaged person will have no such debts. Twelfth, a high-level task force can be created within the U.S. Office of Education to coordinate recommendations suggested below.

1. An availability pool for undergraduate study (an increase in the number of minority high school graduates and an increase in quality of their elementary and high school educational experiences). To improve the number and quality of minority high school graduates for college study we recommend that the federal government provide incentive money to states and local school districts similar to those now provided through the Emergency School Aid Act (ESAA; for school desegregation) to equalize instructional resources and funding among the schools within and between school districts. We recommend that school districts be reimbursed with incentive-type monies for providing equal funding to all schools on a per pupil basis from local and state sources (for example, no school will receive more than 5 percent more or less than another elementary or secondary school within a particular school district). (ESAA Title I and other state, local, and federal compensatory education funds would be excluded from this formula.)

We recommend that a second type of incentive appropriation be established to award local school districts which prepare and counsel minority students to pursue a college education. Therefore, colleges should be required to keep records of minority students by school district who reach their third year of college; and that based upon these records local school districts could be reimbursed incentive monies for the number of students graduating from their districts who reach their junior year in college. We feel that this type of incentive appropriation will provide the necessary motivation for school districts to counsel more minority students in the direction of a career through a college education.

We recommend that a special grant enrollment program funded by the federal government should be established for minority students who wish to attend the more selected institutions of higher education such as the major universities. Our study reveals that minorities are underrepresented at high-status institutions such as universities and graduate centers; thus, we feel that this kind of incentive is needed in order to increase the number and percentage of minority students at the more prestigious universities and graduate centers. We recommend that these grants be made available to minority students who wish to matriculate at those institutions regardless of their academic background and/or economic status. These grants should be aimed only at disadvantaged minority students. The goal here should be to increase minority representation at high-status institutions, not necessarily to increase a percentage of minority students for economically and/or educationally disadvantaged background.

2. An availability pool for graduate and professional schools. To increase the availability pool of minority students for graduate schools, we offer this recommendation to increase the number and quality of undergraduate education for minorities. We recommend that colleges and universities be provided incentive monies and be so reimbursed for the number of minority graduates who are admitted to graduate and professional programs. We feel that this type of financial incentive will do two things: (1) it will encourage colleges and universities to counsel minority students to enter graduate studies, and (2) it will serve to increase the quality of the offerings and services provided minority students during their undergraduate years.

We recommend that special grants and loans be established to provide financial assistance for those minority students who wish to pursue a graduate or professional program of study in areas where minorities are critically underrepresented, such as educational psychology, anthropology, archaeology, nuclear medicine, agricultural sciences, and geology. We feel that this type of incentive program is needed in order to gain a more even distribution of minority graduate students across all disciplines. We recommend that the critical area for minorities be based upon their representation within the various graduate and professional schools. For example, while Hispanic Americans and blacks may be underrepresented in the sciences, the same may not be true for Asian Americans. An incentive program for Asian Americans might be to increase their enrollment within the behavioral and social sciences; while one for blacks and Hispanic Americans might be designed to increase their enrollment within the physical and biological sciences.

3. Equal educational opportunity based upon an equal availability of funds. Two criteria must be met in this country in order to attend college: first, a qualified high school graduate must gain admittance to the college of his choice; second, he must have the funds required to attend that institution. The federal government must also address itself to the latter; it must provide an opportunity for every qualified high school graduate in this country with the desire to attend college to do so. That is, the government must provide the necessary combination of grants, loans, and fellowships for those who need financial assistance.

Increased funding must be a priority rather than "going along with" the phasing-down of college work-study, direct loans, and supplemental educational opportunity grants. Individually geared funding should be allocated as a result of a needs assessment which allows for student aid programs which are institutionally based as well as those that transmit funds directly to students. Supplemental funding should be allocated to those institutions with a proven record of educating and granting degrees to low-income minorities rather than just enrolling them. This might be in the way of an incentive grant for proven performance, as well as graduate-school admittance.

4. Curricula reform. We recommend that special appropriations be put aside to stimulate curricula reform at institutions of higher education. During the late 1960s and early 1970s much of the minority student unrest on college campuses was the result of attempts to infuse into the regular disciplines (mainly the social sciences, for example, sociology, political science, education, anthropology, and history) new subject matter for discussion and new methodologies. Therefore, we recommend that special programs within the U.S. Office of Education should be established to provide incentive monies, upon application from institutions, to promote curricula reform in the social and behavioral sciences; and to promote special cultural and bilingual educational programs at our colleges and universities. We feel strongly that a certain amount of curricula reforms are needed to include the many concerns of minority students; and we feel that the federal government should take the initiative through incentive-type legislation and appropriations to provide the impetus for this reform.

5. A higher education equal opportunity task force. We recommend that a high-level task force be created within the U.S. Office of Education, designed specifically to carry out the recommendations suggested above. We further recommend that this task force be advised by a presidentially appointed committee composed of interested parties from throughout the country. The committee will advise the special task force on the drafting of specific programs, appropriate legislation, and appropriation measures that will have to be approved and funded by the U.S. Congress. Without this special task force and liaison committee we feel that our suggestions will be more difficult to achieve.

6. Research. "Minority" projects supported by federal funds and allocated to major agencies must be carefully monitored and evaluated. These projects should be evaluated with one major criterion, largely determinant of achievement. This criterion must be that of expanding knowledge and research needed to achieve parity and open access to all higher education opportunities for minorities. More minority researchers should be involved in institutions directly involved in the development of policy-oriented research.

The present funding guidelines and policies are discriminatory as they relate to training and research. Whether a program is labeled training or research determines the level of administrative costs. Those programs which are fortunately labeled "research" follow the standard process of being reimbursed for all indirect costs; while those unfortunate enough to be designated as "training" have a maximum of 8 percent for indirect costs. The majority of programs which focus on minorities and the disadvantaged are nonresearch and therefore are labeled as training programs, thereby discriminating against those institutions that have made a programmatical and curricular thrust to serve the disadvantaged. This practice clearly illustrates the pitfalls of state and federal government funding which evaluate research-related activities more positively than human resource activities.

We have excluded from our list of specific recommendations those that are designed for local and state governments. However, we do not wish to imply that state and local efforts are not important sources for improving the enrollment of minority students in institutions of higher education. We recognize that major efforts thus far have emanated from local and state sources via upward bound programs, equal opportunity programs, and other state and local compensatory educational programs aimed at improving minority college enrollment. On the other hand, we feel that the major impetus and motivation in this area should come from the federal government via incentive-type programs designed to increase the availability pool of minority students for undergraduate education, to improve the quality of elementary and secondary schooling for minority-group members, and to improve the "availability pool" among minority group members for graduate and professional studies.

We feel that these recommendations are fundamental to the notion of social justice and equality under the law: everyone should have an equal chance. Further, like the automobile, elementary and secondary education is a necessity for the nation's survival. Minorities should and can play a vital role in helping the nation to survive.

Astin, Alexander. 1975. Preventing Students from Dropping Out. San Francisco: Jossey-Bass Publishers.

Astin, Alexander W. 1971 (Winter). New Evidence on Campus Unrest. Educational Record, pp. 41-46.

_____ and Bayer, Allen E. 1971. Antecedents and Consequents of Disruptive Campus Protests. Measurement and Evaluation in Guidance, April, pp. 18-30.

Ballard, Allen B. 1973. The Education of Black Folk. New York: Harper and Row, pp. 42-44.

Blauch, Lloyd and Jenkins, Martin D. 1942. National Survey of the Higher Education of Negroes--Intensive Study of Selected Colleges for Negroes 3, no. 6. U.S. Office of Education.

Boyd, II, William. 1974. Desegregating America's Colleges and Universities. New York: Praeger.

Brown, Ina C. 1942. National Survey of the Higher Education of Negroes--Socio-Economic Approach to Educational Problems no. 6. U.S. Office of Education.

Carnegie Commission. 1973. The Purposes and the Performances of Higher Education in the United States Approaching the Year 2000. New York: The Commission.

Corcoran, Thomas B. 1973. Community Colleges: The Coming Slums of Higher Education. Change.

Cordasco, Francesco and Bucchioni, Eugene. 1972. The Puerto Rican Community and Its Children on the Mainland. Metuchen, N.J.: Scarecrow Press.

Crossland, Fred E. 1971. Minority Access to College. New York: Ford Foundation.

De Loria, Vine. 1970. We Talk You Listen. New York: Macmillan.

Devall, W. B. 1971 (Winter). Community Colleges: Dissenting View. Educational Record.

Dian, Adolph and Eliades, David K. 1972. The Lumbee Indians and Pembroke State University. The American Indian Reader, ed. Jeannette Henry. San Francisco: The Indian Historical Press, American Indian Educational Publishers.

Erickson, Frederick. 1975 (February). Gatekeeping and the Melting Pot: Interaction in Counseling and Encounters. Harvard Educational Review.

Fallows, Marjorie R. 1975 (March). Community Colleges--Goodby Pygmalion. Change.

Gleazer, Edmund J. 1970. The Community College Issue of 1970s. Educational Record, Winter, pp. 7-52.

Hansen, Donald A. et al. 1972. Socio-Economic Inequities in College Entry: A Critical Specification. American Educational Research Journal 9, no. 4 (Fall).

Hodgkinson, Harold L. 1970. Student Protest--An Institutional and National Profile. Teachers College Record, Spring, pp. 537-55.

Jencks, C. 1968 (Winter). Social Stratification and Higher Education. Harvard Educational Review.

Johnson, Charles S. 1969. The Negro College Graduate. New York: Negro Universities Press.

Karabel, Jerome. 1972. Community Colleges and Social Stratification. Harvard Educational Review 42, no. 4 (November): 521-62.

Lopez, Ronald W. and Enos, Darryl D. 1972. Chicanos and Public Higher Education in California, Parts I and II. ERIC, Ed 071-067, HE-003-803.

Medsker, L. L. and Tillery, D. 1971. Breaking the Access Barrier: A Profile of Two-Year Colleges. New York: McGraw-Hill.

Merian, Lewis et al. 1928. The Problem of Indian Administration. Baltimore: Johns Hopkins University Press.

Mommsen, Kent G. 1974. Black Doctorates in American Higher Education: A Cohort Analysis. Journal of Social and Behavioral Sciences, Spring.

REFERENCES   163

Moore, W., Jr. 1970. Against the Odds--The High Risk Student in
    the Community College. San Francisco: Jossey-Bass.

Pifer, Alan. 1973. The Higher Education of Blacks in the United
    States. Carnegie Corporation of New York.

Rist, R. 1970. Student Social Class and Teacher Expectations:
    The Self-fulfilling Prophecy in Ghetto-Education. Harvard
    Educational Review 40: 411-45.

Rouche, John E. and Kirk, R. W. 1973. Catching Up: Remedial
    Education. San Francisco: Jossey-Bass.

Sillas, Herman (Chairperson). 1975. Asian Americans and Pacific
    Peoples: A Case of Mistaken Identity. California Advisory
    Committee to the U.S. Commission on Civil Rights, February.

Stanford University, Office of Chicano Affairs, Ph.D. List. 1974.
    Spanish Surnamed Americans Holding a Doctorate.

State University of New York. 1976. The 1974-75 Annual Report of
    the Educational Opportunity Program (EOP).

Stent, Madelon D., and Brown, Frank. 1974. Minority Enrollment
    and Representation in Institutions of Higher Education: A Sur-
    vey on Minority Students Enrollment in Colleges, Universities,
    Graduate and Professional Schools in 50 States and District of
    Columbia. New York: Ford Foundation, 1974/ERIC, 1975.

Strauss, Robert P. and Harkins, Peter B. 1974. The 1970 Census
    Undercount and Revenue Sharing: Effect on Allocations in New
    Jersey and Virginia. Washington, D.C.: Joint Center for
    Political Studies.

Taubman, Paul and Wales, Terence. 1974. Higher Education and
    Earnings--College as an Investment and a Screening Device.
    New York: McGraw-Hill.

U.S. Office of Education. 1942. National Survey of the Higher Edu-
    cation of Negroes--General Studies of Colleges for Negroes,
    II, no. 6.

_____. 1974. Projections of Education Statistics to 1982-83.

_____. 1975. U.S. Office of Education Programs Affecting Hispanic Americans. November.

Wright, Stephen J. 1972. Redressing the Imbalance of Minority Groups in the Professions. Journal of Higher Education 43, no. 3 (March).

SELECTED BIBLIOGRAPHY

American Association of Colleges of Pharmacy. "Report on Enrollment in Schools and Colleges of Pharmacy, 1972-73," 1974.

American Bar Association. "Law School and Bar Admission Re-
quirements--A Review of Legal Education in the United States--
Fall 1974." Chicago, 1975.

American Council on Education. The American Freshman: National
Norms for Fall 1974, Cooperative Institutional Research Program, ACE and UCLA (Los Angeles, 1975).

_____. The American Graduate Student: A Normative Description,
ACE Research Report 6, no. 5 (October 1971).

_____. Enrollment of Minority Graduate Students at Ph.D. Graduat-
ing Institutions, August 1974.

_____. Student Assistance Participants and Programs 1974-75,
Higher Education Panel Reports, No. 27 (December 1975).

American Council on Higher Education. Earned Degrees, A Fact
Book on Higher Education, 1972.

American Dental Association. "Minority Report," Dental Education
Supplement No. 4, 1974-75. January 1975.

_____. "Minority Student Enrollment and Opportunities in U.S.
Dental Schools." Annual Report 1972-73 Dental Education
Supplement.

Association of American Medical Colleges. Datagram. Washington,
D.C., 1974.

Astin, Alexander. Preventing Students from Dropping Out. San
Francisco: Jossey-Bass, 1975.

_____ et al. Supplementary National Norms for Freshmen Entering
College in 1966. American Council on Education 2, no. 3
(1967).

Astin, Helen et al. Higher Education and the Disadvantaged Student.
    Washington, D.C.: Human Service Press, 1972.

Aurbach, Herbert A. et al. The Status of American Indian Education,
    A Report to USOE. University Park: Pennsylvania State Uni-
    versity, January 1970.

Bayer, Alan E. The Black College Freshmen: Characteristics and
    Recent Trends. American Council on Education 7, no. 3 (1972).

Blake, Elias Jr. et al. Degrees Granted and Enrollment Trends in
    Historically Black Colleges: An Eight-Year Study. Washing-
    ton, D.C.: Institute for Services to Education, 1975.

Bond, Horace Mann. Black American Scholars. Detroit: Balamp
    Publishing, 1972.

Callahan, Daniel M. and Lake, Dale G. "Changing a Community
    College." Educational Urban Society 6, no. 1 (November
    1973).

College Entrance Education Board. Toward Equal Opportunity for
    Higher Education--Report of the Panel on Financing Low-
    Income and Minority Students in Higher Education. New York,
    1973.

The Chronicle of Higher Education--Fact-File. From U.S. Bureau
    of the Census data, March 22, 1976.

Curtis, James L. Blacks, Medical Schools, and Society. Ann
    Arbor: University of Michigan Press, 1971.

Deloria, Vine Jr. Behind the Trail of Broken Treaties: An Indian
    Declaration of Independence. New York: Delta, 1974.

El-Khawas, Elaine H. and Kinzer, Joan L. Enrollment of Minority
    Graduate Students--at Ph.D. Graduating Institutions. Ameri-
    can Council on Education, August 1974.

Engineering Manpower Commission. Engineering and Technology
    Degrees, 1974. January 1975.

_____. Engineering and Technology Enrollment, Series 1969-73;
    and follow-up survey, August 1974.

_____. Engineering and Technology Graduates, 1969 through 1974 series and follow-up survey, July 1974.

_____. Statistics on Women and Minority Students in Engineering. April 1974.

Epps, Edgar A. Black Students in White Schools. Worthington, Ohio: Charles A. Jones, 1972.

Ferman, Louis A. et al. Negroes and Jobs. Ann Arbor: University of Michigan Press, 1969.

Fichter, Joseph H. Graduates of Predominantly Negro Colleges, Class of 1964. Washington, D.C.: U.S. Department of Health, Education and Welfare, 1966.

Freed, James R. and Goldberg, Louis J. "Factors Affecting the Admission of Minority Students to Schools of Dentistry." Journal of the National Medical Association 66, no. 6 (November 1974).

Fuchs, Estelle and Havighurst, Robert J. To Live on This Earth: American Indian Education. Garden City, N.Y.: Anchor Books, 1973.

"Give It Back to the Indians: Education on Reservation and Off." Carnegie Quarterly, Spring 1969.

Hamilton, I. Bruce. Graduate School Programs for Minority/ Disadvantaged Students. Princeton, N.J.: Educational Testing Service, 1973.

Harris, Seymour. A Statistical Portrait of Higher Education. New York: McGraw-Hill, 1972.

Henry, Jeanette. The American Indian Reader--Education. San Francisco: American Indian Educational Publishers, 1972.

Hill, Wendell T. and McClain, P. Ronald. "Education Needs of the Black Pharmacy Student." Journal of the American Pharmaceutical Association NS13, no. 2 (February 1973).

Homstrom, Engin I. "Older" Freshmen: Do They Differ from "Typical" Undergraduates? American Council on Education 8, no. 7 (1973).

Huff, Shelia. "Credentialing by Tests or Degrees: Title VII of the
    Civil Rights Act and Griggs V. Duke Power Company."
    Howard Educational Review 44, no. 2 (May 1974).

Ichihashi, Yamato. Japanese in the United States. New York: Arno
    Press and the New York Times, 1969.

Inge, Rosalind R. "Goals of Black College Students." Urban League
    Review 1, no. 1 (Spring 1975).

Institute for Services to Education. Degrees Granted and Enrollment
    Trends in Historically Black Colleges: An Eight-Year Study 1
    no. 1. Washington, D.C.: October 1974, pp. 37 and 48.

Institute for the Study of Educational Policy. Equal Educational Op-
    portunity for Blacks in U.S. Higher Education, An Assessment.
    Washington, D.C.: Howard University Press, 1976.

Jaffe, A. J. Negro Higher Education in the 1960's. New York:
    Praeger, 1968.

Johnson, Willis L. Directory of Special Programs for Minority
    Group Members, 1974. Garrett Park, Md.: Garrett Park
    Press, 1973.

Journal of the American Medical Association 231 (January 1975).

Kung, S. W. Chinese in American Life. Seattle: University of
    Washington Press, 1962.

Lee, Rose Hum. The Chinese in the United States of America.
    London: Oxford University Press, 1960.

Locke, Patricia. A Survey of College and University Programs for
    American Indians. Boulder, Colo.: Western Interstate Com-
    mission for Higher Education, July 1973.

Lopez, Ronald W. et al. Chicanos in Higher Education: Status and
    Issues. Los Angeles: Chicano Studies Center Publications,
    UCLA, Monograph no. 7, 1976.

Lyman, Stanford. Chinese Americans. New York: Random House,
    1974.

Lyons, James E. "Issues in Predicting Black Student Success in Higher Education." Journal of Negro Education 43, no. 4 (Fall 1974).

Mack, Faite. "Educational Opportunity Program Graduates Compared to Educational Opportunity Program Non-Graduates." Journal of Negro Education 43, no. 1 (Winter 1974).

National Research Council/National Academy of Sciences. Doctoral Scientists and Engineers in the United States, 1973 Profile. March 1974.

_____. Summary Report 1973 Doctorate Recipients from United States Universities. Washington, D.C., May 1974.

Nava, Julian. Viva La Raza! New York: Van Nostrand, 1973.

"Opportunities for Engineering Graduates 1974-1984." Engineering Education, April 1, 1974.

Padulo, Louis et al. Minorities in Engineering--A Blueprint for Action. New York: The Alfred P. Sloan Foundation, 1974.

Pands, Robert J. et al. National Norms for Entering College Freshmen, Fall 1967. American Council on Education 2, no. 7 (1967).

Parry, Mary Ellen. A Survey of Programs for Disadvantaged Students in Graduate Schools. Princeton, N.J.: Educational Testing Service, February 1970.

Peck, David. "The American Indian and Higher Education." Journal of Social and Behavioral Sciences 20, no. 1 (Winter 1974).

Ramirez, Manuel III and Castanedz, Alfredo. Cultural Democracy, Bicognitive Development, and Education. New York: Academic Press, 1974.

Rivas, Gilberto Lopez y. The Chicanos. New York: Monthly Review Press, 1973.

Schudson, Michael. "Organizing the Meritocracy: A History of the College Entrance Examination Board." Howard Educational Review 42, no. 1 (February 1972).

Smith, Barbara Lee and Hughes, Anita L. "'Spillover' Effect of the Black Educated: Catalysts for Equality." Journal of Black Studies 4, no. 1 (September 1973).

State University of New York. "The 1974-75 Annual Report of the Educational Opportunity Program (EOP)" revised. Albany, 1976.

Statistical Abstract of the United States, 1972. Population statistics are from 1970 Census data.

Szasz, Margaret. "Thirty Years Too Soon: Indian Education Under the Indian New Deal." Integrated Education, July 1975.

Taylor, Theodore W. States and Their Indian Citizens. Washington, D.C.: U.S. Department of Interior, 1972.

Tinto, Vincent. "College Proximity and Rates of College Attendance." American Educational Research Journal 10, no. 4 (Fall 1973).

_____. "Dropout from Higher Education: A Theoretical Synthesis of Recent Research." Review of Educational Research 45, no. 1 (Winter 1975).

U.S. Bureau of the Census. Census of the Population, 1970.

_____. "Characteristics of American Youth: 1974." Special Studies, Series P-23 No. 51. Washington, D.C.: U.S. Government Printing Office, 1975.

_____. Characteristics of the Population, 1970.

_____. "Detail Characteristics of the Population," 1970, United States and California, Florida, Illinois, New York, Texas, and "Special Subject Reports."

_____. Current Population Reports. "Characteristics of the Low-Income Population: 1973." Washington, D.C.: U.S. Government Printing Office, 1975, Table 47.

_____. "Income and Expenses of Students Enrolled in Postsecondary Schools: October 1973." Series P20, No. 281. Washington, D.C.: U.S. Government Printing Office, 1975, Table I, Table E, and p. 4.

_____. Persons of Spanish Origin in the United States: March 1974.
Washington, D.C.: U.S. Government Printing Office, 1975,
Table 1 and pp. 38-39.

_____. Persons of Spanish Origin in the United States, March 1975.
Series P-20, No. 280. Washington, D.C.: U.S. Government
Printing Office, Tables 1, 2, 6, and A.

_____. School Enrollment--Social and Economic Characteristics of
Students: October 1974. Series P-20, No. 278. Washington,
D.C.: U.S. Government Printing Office, 1975.

_____. Social and Economic Characteristics of Students: October
1973. Series P-20, No. 272. Washington, D.C.: U.S.
Government Printing Office, 1974, p. 2.

_____. The Social and Economic Status of the Black Population in
the United States, 1974. Special Studies Series P-23, No. 54.
Washington, D.C.: U.S. Government Printing Office, 1975,
Tables 23, 39, 66, 69, and 71, and p. 25.

_____, Subject Reports. American Indians in the U.S. PC (2) IF,
June 1973, Table II.

_____. Educational Attainment. PC (2) - 5B, March 1973.

_____. Japanese, Chinese, and Filipinos in the United States.
PC (2) - 1G, July 1973.

_____. Negro Population. PC (2) - 1B, May 1973.

_____. Persons of Spanish Origin. PC (2) - 1C, June 1973, Table 1.

_____. Persons of Spanish Surname. PC (2) - 1D, June 1973.

_____. Puerto Ricans in the United States. PC (2) - 1E, June 1973,
Table 1.

_____. School Enrollment. PC (2) - 5A, April 1973.

U.S. Commission on Civil Rights. The Federal Civil Rights Enforcement Effort--1974. Vol. III: To Ensure Equal Educational Opportunity. January 1975.

_____. Towards Quality Education for Mexican Americans. Report VI: Mexican American Education Study, February 1974.

U.S. Department of Health, Education and Welfare. Digest of Educational Statistics, 1975 ed. Washington, D.C.: U.S. Government Printing Office, 1976, Table 90.

_____. "Earned Degrees Conferred 1972-73 and 1973-74," Summary Data. Washington, D.C.: U.S. Government Printing Office, 1976, Table 5.

_____. Fall Enrollment in Higher Education 1972, 1974.

_____. Federal Agencies and Black Colleges, Fiscal Year 1971, OE 73-01 300, 1973.

_____. "Institutions of Higher Education, 1970, Constituent Institutions, 1970." Report BI Final, Unpublished, Table II-36A.

_____, Office for Civil Rights. "Racial and Ethnic Enrollment Data from Institutions of Higher Education, Fall 1974." 1976, Table II-43A.

_____, Office of Education. National Center for Education Statistics. Educational Statistics, 1972.

_____, Office of Student Assistance, BPE Division of Student Support and Special Programs. Program Support Branch, 1976, Unpublished.

U.S. Department of the Interior, Bureau of Indian Affairs. Career Development Opportunities for Native Americans, 1975.

_____. Indian Education: Steps to Progress in the 70's. 1975.

_____, Office of Indian Education Programs. Fiscal Year 1973 and 1974 Statistics Concerning Indian Education. Washington, D.C.: U.S. Government Printing Office, 1975.

U.S. Department of Justice, Immigration and Naturalization Service. 1972 Annual Report.

Vazquez, Hector I. Discrimination Against Puerto Rican Professionals and Puerto Rican Pupils in New York City Public Schools. New York: Puerto Rican Forum, January 27, 1971.

Wells, Robert N. and Sandstrom, Roy H. The American Indian
    Student in Higher Education. Canton, N.Y.: St. Lawrence
    University, July 1972.

admittance to graduate school, 144

associate degrees earned, by race, 59-63

attendance at Bureau of Indian Affairs schools, 23, 26, 27

availability pool, 33

bachelor's degrees earned, by race, 59

Basic Educational Opportunity Grant program (BEOG), 133

Bureau of Indian Affairs schools, 23

change, ability to effect, 143

Chicano student, 146

Chinese Exclusion Act, 39

college, definition of: two-year, 7; four-year, 7

college age population, by race, 31

College Work-Study program (CWS), 135

congressional acts: Cable Act of 1932, 40; Chinese Exclusion Act of 1882, 39; Immigration Act of 1965, 40; Indian Reorganization Act of 1934, 40; Japanese Exclusion Act of 1924, 39; Toidings-McDuffie Act of 1934, 40; War Brides Act of 1946, 40; War Brides Act (amended) of 1947, 40

cost of undergraduate education: private institution, 124; public institution, 124

data: major sources, 8; strengths, 9; weaknesses, 9

definition of terms, 7

degrees, 59, 60, 63, 66, 103; bachelor's, 63, 78; doctor's, 82; master's, 82

degrees conferred by black colleges, 35, 63

degrees earned in: Afro-American studies, 63; biological sciences, 64, 65; business and management, 64, 65; education, 64, 65; engineering, 69-81, 97; Mexican American cultural studies, 63; Native American cultural studies, 63; pharmacy, 78, 81; physical sciences, 64, 65; social sciences, 64, 65; urban studies, 66

doctorate degrees, field of study, 103

earning and schooling, 14

economic assistance: federal, 124, 127, 130, 133, 135; private, 124, 130, 135; state, 127, 130, 135, 136

educational attainment: black, 14, 16, 96; Chinese, 16; Cuban origin, 16; Filipino, 16; Hawaiian, 16; Hispanic American, 16, 55, 58, 96; Japanese, 16; Mexican origin, 16; Native American, 27; Puerto Rican, 16; white, 96

education and income, 14, 16

education of minority groups,
by group (see, student enrollment)
Educational Opportunity Program (EOP), 135
employment status, 116
engineering degrees by curriculum, 72, 74
engineering degrees earned by
blacks, 77
enrollment: by race (see, student enrollment); by sex,
36; by state: California,
105; Florida, 107; Illinois,
109; New York, 111; Texas,
113
enrollment status and family
income, 118

finance and social life, 143
financial assistance, students,
121, 122, 123, 125, 126,
128, 130, 134
financial assistance: characteristics of students, 126;
percentage of students, 128
financial assistance, by race,
federal, 134
financial assistance programs,
federal: Basic Educational
Opportunity Grant (BEOG),
127, 133; College Work-Study
(CWS), 127, 134, 135; Guaranteed Student Loan (GSL),
127, 133; National Direct
Student Loan (NDSL), 127,
134, 135; State Student Incentive Grant (SSIG), 127,
135; Supplemental Educa-
tional Opportunity Grant
(SEOG), 127, 133, 134
financial assistance programs,
New York State: Discovery
program, 135; Equal

Opportunity Programs (EOP)
135; Full Opportunity program, 135; Higher Educa-
tional Opportunity Program
(HEOP), 135
financial assistance in New
York, by race, 134
financial assistance, sources:
federal, 127; private, 130,
134, state, 127, 130, 135
four-year institution, 7
full-time equivalent (FTE), 8
full-time students, definition,
7

graduates, Native American,
25
graduate school enrollment,
84, 85
Guaranteed Student Loan Program (GSL), 133

Higher Educational Opportunity
program (HEOP), 135
Hispanic American population,
by race: black/Negro, 48;
Filipino, 48; Indian, 48;
other, 48; white, 48
Hispanic American under-
graduate enrollment: all
Spanish, 53, 54; Mexican
Americans, 53, 54; Puerto
Rican American, 53, 54

immigrant population: China
and Taiwan, 40; Japan, 40;
Korea, 40; Philippines, 40;
Western Samoa, 40
income, black student, 14, 15,
117, 118, 119; family, 85,
118; source of, 125, 126,
128, 130, 132, 133, 134,
135, 136; Hispanic Ameri-
can student, 120; white
student, 117, 118, 119

income of males and schooling,
    14
Indians: Choctaw, 22; Lumbee,
    22
Indian Reorganization Act of
    1934, 23

lower division, 8
low-income level, 119, 120

median family income, by race,
    117
Mexican American (see, Chicano
    student)
migrant programs, 47
minority enrollment: by degree
    of level, 70, 71, 74, 75, 77;
    by field of study, 72, 73, 74,
    84, 90, 94, 100
minority enrollment in: arts
    and humanities, 84, 100; bio-
    logical sciences, 84, 100;
    business, 84, 100; dental
    school, 87, 89, 100; educa-
    tion, 84, 100; engineering,
    70, 71, 84, 100; law school,
    94, 95, 100; medical school,
    89, 90, 92, 100; pharmacy,
    79; physical sciences, 84,
    100
minority programs, 116, 145

National Direct Student Loan
    program (NDSL), 135
Native American enrollment:
    elementary, 22, 23; second-
    ary, 22, 23; college, 26,
    27, 114

pharmacy enrollment, by race,
    79
population: Chinese, 40, 41;
    Hispanic American, 45,
    46, 47; Native American, 21;
    Puerto Rican, 48

population, college age: all
    races, 32, 33, 34;
    black, 32, 33, 34; white,
    32, 33, 34
professional occupation:
    dentists, 19; engineers, 19;
    lawyers and judges, 19;
    life and physical scientists,
    19; physicians, 19; teachers,
    19
professional occupation, by
    race: Asian American and
    others, 81; blacks, 19, 81;
    Chinese, 81; Filipino, 81;
    Hispanic American, 19, 81;
    Japanese, 81; Native Ameri-
    can, 81; whites, 19
professional schools: dental,
    86, 87; graduate, 83, 84,
    85, 114; law, 93, 94, 95;
    medical, 88-93
profile, statistical, 97

reports: Carnegie Commis-
    sion on Higher Education,
    151; Merian, 23
resident undergraduate, 8

schools (see, professional
    schools)
schooling and earning (see,
    earning and schooling)
schooling completed by Hispanic
    Americans, 54
social life, 144
socioeconomic status, 8
source and amount of funding,
    graduate: private, 125,
    130, 134; public, 125, 130,
    134; undergraduate: private,
    125, 130, 134; public, 125,
    130, 134
Standard Metropolitan Statis-
    tical Areas (SMSAs), 8

State Student Incentive Grant
    program (SSIG), 133
statistical profile of persons
    receiving doctor's degrees,
    97
student: enrollment, 141;
    finance and social life, 143;
    social life, 143, tutoring, 143,
    unrest, 140
student enrollment, by race:
    Asian, 39, 40, 43, 60; black
    American, 14, 17, 26, 27, 37,
    69, 144; black college, 29, 33,
    37; Cuban origin, 14; Filipino,
    14, 39; graduate, 105, 107,
    111, 113, 145; Hawaiian, 14;
    Hispanic American, 17, 45,
    46, 47, 52, 53, 54, 55;
    Japanese, 14; Mexican ori-
    gin, 14, 36; minority, 100;
    Native American, 14, 17,
    24, 25, 26, 27, 36, 60, 110;
    Oriental, 36; Spanish sur-
    name, 14, 53, 54, 55, 60;
    undergraduate, 25, 26, 27
Supplemental Educational Op-
    portunity Grant program
    (SEOG), 133

Third World, 142
Toidings-McDuffie Act of 1934,
    40

Treaty of Guadalupe Hidalgo,
    45
tutoring, 143

undergraduate enrollment, by
    race (see, student enroll-
    ment)
underrepresentation, 8
unemployment: black, 117;
    white, 117
Upward Bound program, 194
unrest, student, 140
urban studies, 66

veterans, 38, 55
veterinary medicine, 119, 129

War Brides Act, 40
women: Asian, 41; engineer-
    ing, 76; enrollment, 36;
    law, 97
white: college population, 32;
    degrees, undergraduate,
    59-62; disadvantaged, New
    York, 129; doctoral degrees,
    97, 98, 101; enrollment,
    graduate, 83-85; enrollment,
    selective states, 105-15, en-
    rollment, undergraduate, 17,
    32-37, 56; ethnicity, 2, 48-51;
    income, 117, 118, 119; occupa-
    tions, 19 [law, 95; medical, 92]

ABOUT THE AUTHORS

FRANK BROWN, Associate Professor of Educational Administration, The State University of New York at Buffalo, is an expert in urban and minority education.

Before joining the SUNY at Buffalo, Professor Brown lectured in Teacher Education at the University of California at Berkeley and taught urban education at the City College of New York. He also served as Associate Director of the Fleischman Commission staff, which conducted a three-year study of New York State's schools.

Professor Brown received his Ph.D. in educational policy, planning, and administration from the University of California at Berkeley. Dr. Brown is also author or co-author of several books, and more than a dozen articles dealing with minority education which have been published in such professional journals as Educational Forum, The Journal of Negro Education, Journal of Black Studies, Integrated Education, Urban Education, Law and Education, and Planning and Changing.

MADELON DELANY STENT, Professor of Education and Director of The Institute for Educational Studies and Development at City College, City University of New York, is well known for her expertise in higher education as it relates to cultural pluralism and curriculum development. Professor Stent was the founder and first President of Urban Ed, Inc., one of the country's first minority owned educational research corporations. She has been Director of the North-east Technical Assistance Team, Right-To-Read, U.S.O.E., and has served as a consultant and editor with Random House and Knopf publishers.

When visiting Professor at Fordham University, she was selected to direct the Trainers-of-Trainers of Teachers Project; this work led to publication of Cultural Pluralism: A Mandate for Change in American Education which she co-authored. Professor Stent was also the Director of the research team which authored The Ford Foundation study, Minority Enrollment and Representation in Institutions of Higher Education. Professor Stent also taught at Teachers College, Columbia University and Queens College, C.U.N.Y.

Dr. Stent received her Ed.D. degree in Higher Education, Curriculum and Teaching from Columbia University. Designated a Rockefeller Scholar in 1975, Professor Stent has authored and co-authored numerous articles in the areas of minority relations, research and education.

MALE AND FEMALE GRADUATE STUDENTS:
The Question of Equal Opportunity
                                        Lewis C. Solmon

PLURALISM IN A DEMOCRATIC SOCIETY
                            edited by Melvin M. Tumin
                            and Walter Plotch

A SURVEY OF PUERTO RICANS ON THE U.S.
MAINLAND IN THE 1970S
                            Kal Wagenheim

WOMEN IN ACADEMIA: Evolving Policies Toward
Equal Opportunities
                            edited by Elga Wasserman
                            Arie Y. Lewin
                            and Linda H. Bleiweis

WOMEN'S INFERIOR EDUCATION: An Economic Analysis
                            Blanche Fitzpatrick

THE WORLD'S STUDENTS IN THE UNITED STATES:
A Review and Evaluation of Research on Foreign
Students
                            Seth Spaulding
                            Michael Flack